The Illustrated Library of SACRED IMAGINATION

General Editor : Jill Purce

David Coxhead and Susan Hiller

dreams

Visions of the night

with 110 illustrations, 24 in colour

CROSSROAD · NEW YORK

In this series the images and symbols of the
spiritual journey are explored in word and
picture, colour and form. Ancient knowledge,
eternal myth and lost traditions become a new
resource for the human venture. Some of today's
most important religious authors undertake
vision quests and discover authentic sources of
enlightenment and wholeness in oft forgotten
ways. This series constantly and directly points
the spiritually thirsty seeker to the sacred well of
the soul. For there in the heart dwells the creative
imagination. Art and architecture, nature
patterns and life cycles, mystics and their
discoveries become the key to contemplative
living.

© 1976 David Coxhead and Susan Hiller

The Crossroad Publishing Company
18 East 41st Street, New York, NY 10017

Library of Congress Catalog Card Number
81–67704

Printed in the Netherlands

Visions of the night

The sleeping dreamer

In the beginning, the Word gave origin to the Father.

A phantasm, nothing else existed in the beginning; the Father touched an illusion, he grasped something mysterious. Nothing existed. Through the agency of a dream our Father Nai-mu-ena (he who is, or has, a dream) kept the mirage of his body, and he pondered long and thought deeply.

Nothing existed, not even a stick to support the vision: our Father attached the illusion to the thread of a dream and kept it by the aid of his breath. He sounded to reach the bottom of the appearance, but there was nothing. Nothing existed.

Then the Father again investigated the bottom of the mystery. He tied the empty illusion to the dream thread and pressed the magical substance upon it. Then by the aid of his dream he held it like a wisp of raw cotton.

Then he seized the mirage bottom and stamped upon it repeatedly, sitting down at last on his dreamed earth.

In this myth, which is a psychic and spiritual reality for the Uitoto Indians of Colombia, the creation of the world is achieved through the action of a dream. First there is the Word, the soundless sound, the beginning of Nothingness. From this non-existence, the Father, the Cosmic body, appears as pure Being. He is the Creator: 'Those who have dreamed into the Cosmic dimensions have been creators of the great systems'; out of his own Being, he maintains the illusion and ties it to the dream, presses the magical substance (which is consciousness) to the illusion, and the world comes into existence. It is a reality: he is able to sit down on his own dreamed earth.

The order of dreaming described here, which composes the nature of the reality in which we exist, in which the whole world exists, is certainly not what is usually meant by dreaming. If creation can be the dream of an awakened dreamer, what is the dream state?

Dreaming is a universal experience. It was once believed that not everyone dreamed, and that even those who did dreamed only occasionally. Since Aserinsky and Kleitman's discovery in 1953 of the occurrence of rapid eye movements (REM) in sleep, however, and their recognition that this activity is associated with dreaming, we have known that everyone experiences the dream state with nightly regularity.

We fall asleep and before we wake again, we spend three or four periods, each increasing in length – a total of one and a half hours on average – dreaming. Allowing for the fact that babies dream far more than adults, a human being spends approximately four and a half years of his life in the dream state. But apart from defining the onset and termination of the dream, the biology of dreaming does not help us to understand the experience.

Unlike states of awareness attained through esoteric disciplines by study and technique, we do not need to learn anything to begin to dream. Nor do we need to absorb any chemical to trigger the experience of dreaming. In this sense, the dream state, like the waking state, simply is. It happens as we happen. It seems to be as real as we are; and in this seeming reality lies a basic paradox for the sleeping dreamer.

The objects and actions in our dreams are no less real to us, as we experience them, than the objects in our waking life seem when we are awake. This paradox was expressed more than a thousand years ago by Chuang-tzu: 'One night, I dreamed I was a butterfly, fluttering here and there, content with my lot. Suddenly I awoke and I was Chuang-tzu again. Who am I in reality? A butterfly dreaming that I am Chuang-tzu, or Chuang-tzu dreaming he was a butterfly?'

The problem depends upon our definition of reality. If we experience the dream as real while we are dreaming, but believe that it is unreal when we awake, this is partly because, as sleeping dreamers, we are not conscious in our dreams and so have no point of view from which to see the wholeness of the reality that surrounds us.

Carlos Castaneda explains in one of his Socratic dialogues with don Juan:
'My argument was that the whole event could not have been a battle of power because it had not been real.

"And what is real?" don Juan asked me very calmly.

"This, what we're looking at, is real," I said, pointing to the surroundings.

"But so was the bridge you saw last night, and so was the forest and everything else."

"But if they are real, where are they now?"

"They are right here. If you had enough power you could call them back. Right now, you cannot do that because you think it is very helpful to keep on doubting and nagging. It isn't, my friend, it isn't. There are worlds upon worlds, right here in front of us."'

The spiritual philosophies of India teach that there are many levels of consciousness and not a single, simple reality, as materialist philosophy would have us believe. In a similar way, the psychologist Charles Tart has suggested that what is usually called dreaming may not be one single state, but a number of qualitatively very different states – or altered states of consciousness (ASC), as he calls them – within the matrix of sleep. If this is so, then the ordinary dream, the sleeping dream, is only the beginning, the first level, in a complex multi-levelled dream world.

The world begins: it begins as a dream of Nai-mu-ena in South America, and as a dream of Brahma in the mythology of India. For native Australians, the Dreaming, or the Dreamtime, is the entire mythical past, the present, and the future of Being: nothing that does not exist in the Dreaming, is. One can align oneself with reality only by performing the actions and ceremonies of this mythic, and consequently more real, time outside of time.

Mircea Eliade, on the other hand, has argued in his theory of myth that 'the homology of the persons and events of a myth with those of a dream does not imply any fundamental identity between them'. But this homology can be perceived only because myths are themselves dreams, great dreams whose reality is of a numinous order. As Eliade says, the creations of the unconscious are not the 'raw material' of religion and all that religion includes – symbols, myths, rituals, etc. In fact, the reverse is true: the creations of the unconscious as they appear in the dreams of the sleeping dreamer are homologous with the great cultural myths precisely because these myths are conscious dreams of a higher order. For this reason, we can treat both personal dreams and myths as phenomena within the spectrum of the dream state.

There is a statement by a native Australian that

White man got no dreaming
Him go 'nother way
White man, him go different.

But we *can* learn to dream. And if most of us cannot see the reality of the worlds 'right here in front of us', perhaps we can begin to learn by experience. Ultimately, it may turn out that the reality of these worlds is yet another illusion, and that, to quote Chuang-tzu again, 'Confucius and you are both dreams, and I who say you are a dream am a dream myself. This is a paradox. Tomorrow a wise man may explain it.' As Bhagwan Shree Rajneesh has written, 'Dreaming is one of the greatest subjects. It is still undiscovered, unknown, hidden. It belongs to the secret knowledge. But now the moment has come when everything which is secret must be made open, and everything which was hidden up to now must not now be hidden.'

The science of dreams

While Hermes is leading the souls of the dead to the other world, he passes the *demios oneiron*, the village of dreams. In the Odyssey, the site is located in the outer reaches of Okeanos, on the frontier of the real world. For the pre-Homeric Greeks, the cosmos was organized as a series of concentric circles, receding both in time and in space from the centre, the known and rational world which was ruled by Zeus. Outside the centre were the barbarous lands of strange and uncouth customs; then came the mythical lands where monstrosities and fantastic beings lived, but which also contained the Isles of the Blessed in the eternal Golden Age; beyond this was Okeanos; and beyond this, only the anti-world, the realm of the dead. These circles were at once bands of time and space, the outer being both earlier in time and more distant in space, and the centre being the here and now. In Greek mythical geography, dreams existed at the outer limits of the real world, and close to its beginnings. But since the centre, the known world, was ruled by Zeus, dreams, although by nature obscure and archaic, arrived only as clear messages from him or another of the gods. The Greeks were visited by dreams; they did not 'have' them.

According to Orphic doctrines, the first principle of the cosmos was Chronos, Time, out of which came Chaos, symbolizing the Infinite, and Ether, symbolizing the Finite. Chaos was surrounded by Night which formed the enveloping cover under which cosmic matter was slowly formed by the creative action of the Ether. Finally this universe took the shape of an egg with Night as the shell. In the centre of this gigantic egg, whose upper section formed the vault of the sky and whose lower section was the earth, the first being, Phanes, Light, was born. Night later gave birth to Moros (evil fate), Ker (doom), Thanatos (death), Hypnos (sleep), and to 'the people of dreams'. Morpheus, the god of dreams, was the son of Hypnos. The people of dreams, the images and objects of the dream world, are genealogically closer to primeval origins and have an order of existence prior to the god who rules them. Morpheus rules the world of dreams as we rule our individual dreams. We are responsible for them but their existence is beyond us.

The importance of later Greek philosophies to the understanding of the nature of dreaming lies not so much in specific contributions as in their channelling of ideas inherited from Egypt and the Near East, modified in the tension between their mythic experience of the dream as theophany and their 'modern' search for a rational explanation of the world. From Greece, during the seven hundred years between Heraclitus and Artemidorus, the second-century AD oneirologist, we can trace all the theories of dreaming – materialistic, mystical, analytical, occult and medical – that were available to the west at the beginning of this century.

Homer had already divided dreams into two groups, those that arrived through the Gates of Ivory, and those that came through the Gates of Horn – the true dream and the false. Trying to establish criteria for each became the object of later dream theorists.

While admitting the possibility of divine influence in dreams, Hippocrates, 'the founder of modern medicine', formulated the theory of their diagnostic value. The soul, fully occupied with bodily functions during the waking state, is able, while the body sleeps, to judge the balance of the whole and to perceive in dreams the causes of illness. Thus, as long as dreams are a true representation of waking life, the body is well; but if, for example, the sun turns black in a dream, then there is something wrong with that organ of the body which corresponds on a macrocosmic/microcosmic basis to the real sun.

'The waking have one world in common; sleepers have each a private world of their own,' Heraclitus observed. For him, consciousness is fire, is life, is knowledge; it is at the centre, the light of reason. He considered that both in sleep and in death the soul escapes from the living fire only to founder in moisture. 'It is death for souls to become water.' Dreams, the individual worlds, are still, in a sense, located near Okeanos, in the damp mists of time where consciousness is swamped by the vague unknown.

Aristotle did not believe that dreams are divinely inspired. If dreams were sent by the gods, he argued, they would be received by the best and wisest men, which is not so. Dreams were caused by the 'heart' as the centre of feeling, the centre of all representations, which was affected by minimal organic movements of the body that were obscured by the more violent movements of the senses in the waking state. Because the dreamer is so sensitive to these minimal movements, a skilled dream interpreter can predict illness and prescribe cures from such dreams. It also follows that 'the movements set up first in sleep should also prove to be the starting points of actions to be performed in daytime, since the recurrence by day of the thought of these actions has also had the way prepared for it by the images which came before the mind at night'. Similarly, dreams of close friends can be precognitive because we know them so well that we can predict their actions by assessing their motivations when we are dreaming and more open to subtle information than when awake: 'The most skilful judge of dreams is the man who possesses the ability to detect likenesses: for anyone can judge the vivid dream. . . . Mental pictures are like reflections in water . . . the reflection is not like the original, nor the images like the real object.' Aristotle was also the first philosopher to argue against the likelihood of true precognitive dreams by observing that since there were so many dreams of such variety, some of them were bound to resemble later events.

An alternative theory to the increasingly rationalistic trend represented by Aristotle was held by the Pythagoreans, who believed that in sleep the soul is freed from the body, its tomb, and, soaring upward, is able to perceive and converse with higher beings. This traditional and mystical conception of the dream stems jointly from the Orphic doctrines and from Egypt, where it was believed that the *ba*, or spiritual double, left the physical body during sleep and at death. A similar idea mentioned by Plato, that 'spirits scattered in the etheric regions come to rest near us to imprint on our souls ideas disengaged from the senses, and to transmit to us the orders of God', was expanded by the neo-Platonists from whom it was adopted by the Gnostics, and so passed, via the Renaissance occultists, to the theosophists and later mystics of this century.

Artemidorus of Ephesus wrote that 'dreams and visions are infused into men for their advantage and instruction'. He seems to have been the first Greek to study dreams themselves rather than theories of dreaming: 'I have done nothing neither by day nor night but meditate and spend my spirit in the judgment and interpretation of dreams.' For the first time in the literature of dreams appears a consistent approach based upon observation of 3,000 dreams. Artemidorus' five books of *Oneirocritica* are a Hellenic model of the analytical approach, to which Sigmund Freud was to pay tribute. In order to interpret a dream, Artemidorus insisted, one needed to obtain information about the dreamer: his character and mood, his situation in life, his name. All needed to be known so that the way in which the specific dream related to the particular dreamer could be understood.

Yet despite this concern with the specific dream and the particular dreamer, much of Artemidorus' dream books consists of long lists of dreams divided into categories by subject in a way which, in even more simplistic formats, was to remain popular throughout the western world up to the present day:

'To be blind of both eyes is loss of children, brethren, father and mother. Notwithstanding, this dream is good for him which is in prison and to him which is very poor; for the first shall no more see his evils about him, the second shall have wherewith to aid and pleasure himself, as many are ready to lend their helping hand to the blind. . . . If anyone that is in search of a thing that is lost dreams this dream, he shall never find it. To poets this dream is good, for they have need of great sleep when they would invite verse; to sick persons this dream brings daily expectation of death.'

Despite the decidedly negative judgment of Aristotle, and the generally dismissive attitude towards the ontological status of dreams natural in a society as inchoately rationalistic as Greece, there was great interest in dreams on a popular level. A plethora of dream interpreters and diviners of all kinds succeeded Artemidorus and were able to support themselves by their art. Cultural phenomena exist only insofar as they are usable, and the success of Artemidorus and his followers can only be explained as fulfilling an otherwise unrecorded need.

The history of Israel as recorded in the Historical Books and the Pentateuch of the Old Testament is the biography of Yahveh, and the duty of the Jews was to follow the will of God as it was expressed in the divinely inspired laws, supplemented by the visions and dreams of the prophets: 'If there is a prophet among you, I the Lord will make myself known to him in a vision; I will speak with him in a dream.' When God spoke to the Jews He sent a message that had a mythic–historical significance, and He either spoke directly, as to Jacob, who 'dreamed that there was a ladder set up on the earth . . . and behold the Lord stood above it, and said: I am the Lord, the God of Abraham your father and the God of Isaac; the land on which you lie I will give to you and your descendants' (Gen. 28.12), or His message appeared in dreams so thinly veiled that its meaning was immediately apparent, as in the case of Joseph: 'Hear this dream that I have dreamed: behold, we were binding sheaves in the field, and lo, my sheaf arose and stood upright; and behold, your sheaves gathered around it, and bowed down to my sheaf. His brothers said to him, "Are you indeed to reign over us?"' (Gen. 37.5). Indeed, the validating criterion of theophany was that there was no ambiguity about meaning, and for this reason only Jews – usually kings or prophets – received this sort of dream. The dreams of Gentiles recorded in the Old Testament are always symbolic and must be interpreted with God's help by a Jew, as, for instance, when Joseph interpreted Pharaoh's dream.

It is not that the Jews of the Old Testament did not dream in the same ways in which we dream; but, because of their sense of mythic history, most dreams were of no interest to them. Living as they did as a small aggregate of tribes surrounded by more powerful nations with lively traditions of dream interpretation, magic, and divination, it was precisely their lack of interest in such things which, combined with a strict monotheism, defined and maintained them.

In the poetic and prophetic books, which are not confined within the traditions of orthodox theology, 'God speaks to man in one way, and in two, though man does not perceive it. In a dream, in a vision of the night, when deep sleep falls upon men, while they slumber in their beds, then He opens the ears of men.' (Job 33.12). Spiritual growth is more active in dreams than in the waking state, because we are withdrawn from our own wills. For those who are not able to receive waking visions, God's communications can be more direct in dream: 'For the Lord will command his loving kindness in the daytime, and in the night his song shall be with me.' (Psalm 42.8). It is apparent, too, from Job's criticisms, that this communication with God is a normal nightly event: 'By reason of the multitude of oppressions they cry out; they cry for help by reason of the arm of the mighty. But none saith, Where is God, my maker, who giveth me songs in the night.' Through the medium of the dream, the chosen few hear God's song, until the millennium arrives, when 'I will pour out my spirit on all flesh; your sons and your daughters shall prophesy, your old men shall dream dreams, and your young men shall see visions' (Joel 2.28). Until the millennium, dreams are the special means of receiving divine instruction and inspiration: 'Except the Lord build the house, they labour in vain that build it: Except the Lord keep the city, the watchman waketh in vain. It is vain for you that ye rise early, and so late take rest, and eat the bread of toil: For he giveth unto his beloved in their sleep' (Psalm 127).

In the New Testament, Christ's conception was announced to Joseph in a dream (Matt. 1.20); the same event, however, was revealed directly to Mary while she was awake. These levels of spiritual perception are defined first in the Old Testament when God announces that He will speak to prophets in a dream, but 'My servant Moses is not such . . . with him I will speak mouth to mouth, even manifestly.' Although these biblical dreams have been formalized to accommodate a specific religious tradition, the idea was widespread in the ancient world that the unknown, or God, was more accessible to ordinary people in dreams than in the vision by day, in which a more subtle reality has to compete with and overcome the perceptions of the senses. Waking visions are attained with difficulty and only by those who are by nature already more spiritual.

A curious fragment of older traditions is expressed in the dream concerning the judgment of Jesus by Pilate. It is curious because almost all biblical dreams are fulfilled, for the dreamer usually obeys the divine message. In this instance, before Pilate was due to pass judgment, 'his wife sent word to him; "Have nothing to do with that righteous man, for I have suffered many things because of him today in a dream"' (Matt. 27.19). Pilate's wife was convinced by her dream of the righteousness of Jesus, and her sense of reality forced her to communicate this conviction to her husband. But Pilate remained unmoved, and Jesus was crucified. Perhaps this is a glimpse of another tradition, such as that preserved in the Coptic Church, where Jesus is seen as a powerful magician with the gift of miracles, visions and healing. In the apocryphal Gospel of Nicodemus, after his wife's message has been given to Pilate, the chief priests say to him, 'Did we not say unto you, he is a magician? Behold, he has caused your wife to dream.' Dreaming is here associated with magic and necromancy defined in opposition to truth and a sense of reality. Pilate had no standpoint from which he could judge the 'true' reality; he could not distinguish the Gates of Horn from the Gates of Ivory, and, incapable of deciding, he washed his hands of the judgment.

While the dreams recorded in the Bible are often surprising to the dreamer, they obviously fall within the religious and cultural boundaries of what is possible. But in Acts 10.9, a trance dream of Peter's breaks with his cultural patterns and inspires him to innovate a radical social and religious change. In the dream Peter sees 'the heavens opened and something descending, like a great sheet. . . . In it were all kinds of animals and reptiles and birds of the air. And there came a voice, "Rise Peter, kill and eat." But Peter said, "No, Lord, for I have never eaten anything that is common or unclean." And the voice came to him a second time, "What God has cleansed you must not call common."' This happened three times. While Peter was attempting to interpret his dream, messengers arrived asking him to teach the gospel of Christ to Cornelius, who was a Gentile, and Peter realized that the dream was telling him that despite the old laws, he must preach to the Gentiles: 'God has shown me that I should not call any man unclean or common,' he says.

ISLAMIC
TRADITIONS

Islam is essentially a prophetic religion, and dreaming has influenced its spiritual life from the beginning. The *Lailatal-Miraj*, or Night Journey, Mohammed's great dream of initiation into the mysteries of the cosmos, began as he 'was sleeping between the hills of Safa and Meeva, when the Angel Gabriel approached' leading Elboraq, the half-human silver mare whom Mohammed rides 'in an instant' to Jerusalem, the centre of the world. In Jerusalem, the Prophet converses and prays with Abraham, Moses and Jesus and then, continuing on his journey, flying on Elboraq and led by Gabriel, he passes through the seven celestial spheres, each infused with its own colour, whose esoteric meanings relate to the seven levels of existence (material, vegetable, animal, human; and three more beyond the potential of ordinary human nature), to reach across the oceans of white light and, finally, to approach God. In some versions of the text, Mohammed not only ascends to God, but also descends to the depths of the earth, thus encompassing all of human experience.

In certain esoteric Javanese Muslim teachings, man's correct place in the universe is said to be at the human level: but, overwhelmed by material objects – not by his desire for the objects but, as these Sufis explain, by the material power expressed by 'things' – man presently lives merely at the material level. The seeker's aim is to achieve true human consciousness, and to do this one must first grasp the vegetable, and then the animal level. Temporary visions of vegetable-level consciousness, which, according to the views of different schools, may or may not inhibit one's ability to reach the higher states on a more permanent basis, can be experienced by taking drugs whose essence belongs to that level. Certain dreams, occurring naturally, are understood as a form of divine grace by means of which one can temporarily taste the states above the material level.

Bu'ya Sadiqa, the dreams that Mohammed experienced in the month preceding the revelation of the Koran, appeared in the form of 'isolated, luminous and sonorous impressions'. The Prophet was either unable or unwilling to translate them, and they appear as isolated letters, part of a cryptic alphabet of ecstasy, standing at the beginning of several chapters of the Koran (Chapter II: A,L,M; Chapter VII: A,L,M,S; Chapter XI: A,L,R; etc.). A numerological and esoteric correspondence between letters and numbers exists in Islam, but commentators on the Koran have so far been unable to discover the significance of this series. The authors of the commentary known as *El Jeladain* wrote: 'Only God knows what He meant by these letters.'

At the time of Mohammed no distinction was made between the sleeping dream and the waking vision. It was felt that only the occasion and the personality of the receiver dictated whether this information would come as a vision by day or as a dream by night, and Mohammed received spiritual instruction in both states. Later, under the influence of early medieval Arabic scholarship with its passion for classification, the more orthodox Muslims, that is, those who were concerned rather with the externals of religion than with spiritual experience, tended to evaluate prophecy and prophets in classifications reminiscent of and probably derived from criteria suggested in the Old Testament. A *nabi* is a simple prophet who can see and hear angels in dreams; a *nabi morsal* is the prophet for a group and can see and hear angels while in the waking state; the Six Great Prophets (Adam, Noah, Abraham, Moses, Jesus and Mohammed) are visionaries who reveal a new law, *shariat*, to mankind and to whom the word of God is dictated verbatim by an angel while they are fully awake.

Some support for this ordering of experience might seem to derive from the comments of certain mystics, for example, Avicenna's observation that man's mind is freer by night than by day, and Kobra's 'What the vulgar, because of the vigour of their lower nature, can experience only in dream, the mystic experiences between waking and sleeping.' The viewpoints from which the judgments are made are worlds apart: the classifications are from the world of material scholarship, the comments from the world of spiritual experience.

Certainly, little attention was paid to categories by the visionaries of the esoteric traditions who continued to accept with ease the soul's ability to experience spiritual or ecstatic states in dreams. The following text of Shamsoddin Lahiji, a fifteenth-century Sufi, exemplifies the great tradition of the spiritual dream within Islam:

'I saw myself present in the world of light. Mountains and deserts were a rainbow of coloured light, red, yellow, white, blue. I experienced an overwhelming nostalgia for them. I became as though struck by madness and was carried outside myself by the violence of the presence and of the deep emotion I experienced. Suddenly I saw that Black Light had enveloped the entire universe. . . . Rays of light joined in me and rapidly pulled the whole of my being upward. [Passing through the seven heavens] . . . finally I reached the Sphere of Spheres. There, without quality or dimension, the light of the theophany shone upon me. I saw the Divine Majesty without modality. During this I was completely annihilated to myself, and without consciousness. Then I came back to myself in this world. Once again the Divine Being appeared to me. Once again I was annihilated to myself and placed outside all limitations. Everything happened as though I no longer existed, then I came back to myself in this world. Then the Divine Being reappeared and I again ceased to exist. But once I had found my superexistence in God, I saw that this absolute light was I. Whatever fills the universe is I; other than myself there is nothing. The eternal being, the demiurge of the universe, is I. Everything is subsistent in me.'

Here, as Henry Corbin comments, Lahiji's Black Light reveals the very secret of being, for all existence has a double face, a face of light and a face of darkness. Lahiji has not descended to hell to find the darkness that most men never acknowledge; he has transcended heaven to find the Black Light, the totality of being which most men never imagine: 'The totality of man's being is the face of day and the face of night; the face of light is the shaping of his inessence into an essence by the absolute subject.' It cannot be doubted, whatever the ontological status of the events he describes so vividly, that this dream marked a vital change in Lahiji's life.

In order to establish the reality of their spiritual experiences in dreams and visions, Muslim mystics were led to identify an existent world of images, the *alam al-mithral*, halfway between the material world and the world of intellect. This world of images is not unreal. Henry Corbin, who has studied the *alam al-mithral* and written about it extensively, explains that affirming the existence of the world of images should not be understood as a flight from what we have agreed to call reality but that, on the contrary, too facile a rejection of it may appear very much like a flight from internal reality. The faculty of active imagination, or imaginative consciousness, by which one is able to enter this world, should not be misinterpreted as fantasy. The world of images is not imaginary: one approaches it through a highly trained and specific 'imagination', and the figures and images which inhabit it have an existence of their own. Ibn 'Arabi describes 'this power of active imagination [that] developed in me to the point that it presents my mystic beloved to me visually in a bodily, objective, extramental figure, just as the Angel Gabriel appeared bodily to the eyes of the Prophet'.

The landscapes and figures of the world of images exist in a reality that has been visited by many, and for each it has had a 'sameness'. The visionary dreamer can, if pure enough in intent and provided he or she has reached a sufficient level of spiritual development, add to this world, or explore it further by means of heightened spiritual understanding. And because the faculty used is this 'imagination', there can be no distinction between 'creation' and 'exploration', between 'develop' and 'identify'. The world of images is a dream world which a number of dreamers may visit, and in which they are able to distinguish recognizable forms and images in the same act by which they create them.

ETHNOGRAPHIC
TRADITIONS

The great wealth of dream material that once existed among the non-literate societies of the world has been studied to its death. Of all the ethnologists and anthropologists who collected information concerning these peoples, few were able to understand the world view or metaphysics of those they were studying, or even to see that such a metaphysics existed. Ideas that in the anthropologists' own society were regarded as philosophy, mysticism or theology, were paternalistically dismissed in the ethnographic literature as 'primitive thinking'. Edward Tylor, one of the founders of anthropology, wrote: 'The evidence of visions corresponds with the evidence of dreams in their bearing on primitive theories of the soul. . . . Even in healthy waking life, the savage or barbarian has never learned to make that rigid distinction between subjective and objective, between imagination and reality, to enforce which is one of the main results of scientific education.'

The Senoi, a people living in the jungle of the Central Highlands of Malaysia, led a collective life centred around a complex dream psychology that served to integrate the community and to encourage a high degree of what C. G. Jung described as 'individuation'. Kilton Stewart, who lived with the Senoi in 1935, wrote that 'the absence of violent crime, armed conflict, and mental and physical diseases . . . can only be explained on the basis of institutions which produce a high state of psychological integration and emotional maturity, along with social skills and attitudes which promote creative rather than destructive interpersonal relations'.

The Senoi believed that every person should try to control his or her own dreamed spiritual universe, demanding and receiving the cooperation of all the characters and forces that exist in it. These characters and forces are real. When they are threatening, the dreamer must fight with them, calling for help from the dream images of friends if necessary; dream characters are dangerous only so long as one is afraid of them. If the dreamer succeeds in winning the dream battle, the spirit of the adversary becomes a servant or ally who will be able to help in future dream and waking life.

Each morning, on waking, the family group discusses and analyses the dreams of the previous night. Children are instructed and encouraged in their dream lives just as children are in waking life. When the Senoi boy reports a falling dream, the adult answers with enthusiasm, 'That is a wonderful dream, one of the best dreams a man can have. Where did you fall to? What did you discover? . . . You must relax and enjoy yourself when you fall in a dream. Falling is the quickest way to get in contact with the powers of the spirit world. . . . Soon, when you have a falling dream, you will remember what I am saying . . . and you will feel that you are travelling to the source of the power that has caused you to fall.'

Pleasant dreams are deliberately and consciously continued until they reach a point where something of beauty or use can be brought back to the group on waking. If a man is flying in a dream, for example, he flies on until he meets beings from whom he can learn a song or a skill that he can bring back to his own people. In sexual dreams, the dreamer always continues until orgasm is reached and then asks his dream-lover for a song. He has no fear of expressing love in his dreams to beings who would be forbidden in waking life, a brother or sister, for example, for such dream characters are not aspects of the brother or sister, but psychic entities who have taken this form as a disguise. Similarly, in the case of aggression dreams, if the dream character who threatens a Senoi appears to be the dream image of a friend, it is not really a friend but only a dream person who is disguised in this way.

After the family dream discussion, the Senoi men gather in the council presided over by a *halak*, or shaman, where the dreams of all are discussed and analysed, and the songs and dances that have been gathered are explained and performed. Shamanism, adeptship, 'knowledge', is the goal of all Senoi men, and the designation *halak* is in no sense an office, but a spiritual state that, potentially, can be achieved by anyone.

Senoi dream theory describes the existence of a spiritual body which consists of a primary heart soul, *sengin*, on which life depends, and four secondary souls: *jereg*, centered in the liver, which can project in space and time; *hinum*, breath, which can leave the body in speech or expression; *ruai*, head, which can leave the body during sleep; and *kenlok*, centered in the eye, which controls sensation and ordinary knowledge. To become a shaman, the *ruai* and at least one other soul must be able to leave the body; and to become a *halak* of the highest level, all the souls – except *sengin* which only leaves the body at death – must be able to travel outside the body and cooperate with *ruai* in the dream world. These noncorporeal aspects of being are thus not confined within the manifestation which is an individual Senoi but, projected through thought, dream and speech, interact with distant people and things.

Two American Indian tribes whose culture was essentially concerned with the dream state are the Maricopa of Colorado, and the Iroquois of the Five Nations Confederacy in New York State. There is no doubt, despite Tylor's assertion to the contrary, that the Iroquois were able to distinguish the dream from the waking state, but for them the dream state had a greater ontological reality. In the seventeenth century, Père Fremin, a French Jesuit missionary, wrote that 'properly speaking, they have only a single divinity – the dream. To it they render their submission and follow all its orders with the utmost exactness . . . whatever it may be that they have done in dreams, [they] believe themselves absolutely obliged to execute at the earliest moment. The other nations content themselves with observing those of their dreams which are the more important; but this people, which has the reputation for living more religiously than its neighbours, would think itself guilty of a great crime if it failed in its observance of a single dream. The people think only of that, they talk about nothing else, and all their cabins are filled with their dreams.'

The Iroquois recognized the dream as the language of the soul, and the means by which it expressed its desires. Very much as Freud did, they believed not only that the dream was a wish-fulfilment, but that the dream often disguised these wishes in its own language.

The Iroquois' emphasis on the primacy of the dream over the secondary reality of the waking state appears to be the mirror image of popular western rationalism in which the waking state is seen as a superior reality and the dream as an unreal state during which the computer-like mind merely shuffles waking images. Both are extremes lacking in wholeness.

Like Smohalla, the Nez Perce, who firmly rejected the white man's work ethic with the words, 'My young men shall never work. Men who work cannot dream, and wisdom comes in dreams', and like the author of Psalm 127, the Maricopa Indians believed that success in life depended on the spirit, and that the spiritual is approached through dreaming. Lost Star said, 'Everyone who is prosperous or successful must have dreamed of something. It is not because he is a good worker that he is prosperous, but because he dreamed.' In the dream state, the soul of the dreamer goes out in search of a spirit who will reveal a song or a cure. All Maricopa subscribed in principle to this theory, but in practice only a few attempted the dream journey to seek instruction in poetry or medicine. The path of knowledge was a difficult and sometimes dangerous one, and not every Maricopa had the heart for it. It was a long process, for the information was given to the dreamer by a guardian or teaching spirit in dreams that might stretch over a period of many years. During this time of apprenticeship, the dreamer was never allowed to mention his or her dreams, nor reveal any information obtained in them. Speaking too soon, without sufficient understanding, would anger the guardian, who would abandon the dreamer.

Leslie Spier tells the story of Papago Foot, given to him by his informant:

'Papago Foot, the Kohuana, went into a cave in a butte near Tempe. He smoked one of the [magical] reeds lying there and fell asleep at once. "He just wanted to do it, because he thought that even if he died it would be better than the way he was living, and perhaps he might become a shaman." He dreamed of a human, whom he did not recognize, who came to him, saying he would help him begin. The spirit tied a cobweb from that butte to Tempe Butte, and thence to Four Peaks, to the San Francisco Mountains, thence to . . . Needles. He travelled along that cobweb and had various cures revealed to him at each butte. But he spoke of this to someone too early, so the spirit said, "You have gone just halfway [around the circuit]. I intended taking you all the way around. . . . But since you have told too soon, you have seen only half of what I had to reveal; you can get along with what you have seen." So this man cured bowel trouble. Others always twitted him for telling.'

In India, two separate approaches to dreaming, the Upanishadic, religio-philosophic and metaphysical, and the yogic, spiritual and experiential, have blended to produce unparalleled richness and complexity. For centuries the dream state has been understood as part of the layered structure of the psychic and spiritual universe, and as a potential area of consciousness by means of which the illusion of reality can be experienced and perceived, and ultimately transcended.

In the *Mandukya Upanishad*, which draws together several esoteric Indian traditions, the essential mantra AUM (OM) – the primal sound, and the mantra associated with the highest chakra, the crown centre – is given as a model for the understanding of the homologous levels of consciousness. Each of the letters, A,U,M, and their totality, OM, represents one of the four states of consciousness, the four quarters of *brahman*, universal mind/soul, and the four quarters of the Self, the *atman*.

'The waking state, outwardly cognitive . . . having nineteen mouths, enjoying the gross, the Common-to-all-men', called *vaisvanara*, is the first quarter; this is the sound of A, consensus reality.

'The dreaming state, inwardly cognitive . . . having nineteen mouths, enjoying the exquisite, the Brilliant', called *taijasa*, is the second quarter; this is the sound of U, the reality of the personal spiritual life, the dream state.

'If one asleep desires no desire whatever, sees no dream whatever, that is deep sleep. . . . The deep sleep state is unified, consisting of bliss . . . whose mouth is thought, the Cognitional'; it is called *prajna*, and represents the third quarter; this is the sound of M, the consciousness of undifferentiated unity.

The fourth quarter is said to be 'not inwardly cognitive, not outwardly cognitive, not both-wise cognitive, not a cognition mass, not cognitive, not non-cognitive, unseen, with which there can be no dealing, ungraspable, having no distinctive mark . . . the cessation of development, tranquil, benign, without a second, such they think is the fourth', called *turiya*. This is the sound OM, the conscious Universal mind (the word that was 'at the beginning').

To the central Upanishadic idea that the *atman*, the individual soul, and *brahman*, the world soul, were essentially one – that is, that through true knowledge, the individual could achieve the god-state – the yogic techniques of asceticism and experiment, and the later and perhaps more important Buddhist yoga of psychology and mysticism, were applied. The object of life, indeed, the individual's primary responsibility, was to realize the freedom and immortality of a god: by realizing the illusion, *maya*, of the world – realizing it not philosophically, as in the earlier *Upanishads*, but practically, experientially. The *Mandukya*, a text which Lama Govinda indicates is still used as a precise psychological tool in Tibetan mysticism, describes the dream state as the second stage through which one must pass in order to achieve enlightenment. In common with *vaisvanara*, everyday reality, *taijasa*, the dream state, is described as 'having nineteen mouths', which Sankara explains in a commentary as the five senses (hearing, touch, sight, smell, taste), the five organs of action (speech, handling, locomotion, generation, excretion), the five vital breaths, the sensorium (*manas*), the intellect (*buddhi*), egoism (*ahamkara*), and thinking (*citta*). When awake and when dreaming, we experience the illusion of these 'nineteen mouths'. In this way, Indian tradition recognizes the paradox of the 'reality' of dreams, which parallels the 'reality' of waking life, by ultimately relegating both to the status of illusion.

Understanding that dreams are illusions is more difficult because one is at first tempted to superficially equate their immateriality with illusion, instead of recognizing this immateriality as a further illusion that one must 'penetrate'.

To 'penetrate' each of the three preliminary states of consciousness – waking, dreaming and dreamless sleep – on the path to *turiya*, one must pass through them in complete lucidity, without any discontinuity of consciousness. The specific technique for maintaining this unbroken awareness is *pranayama*, breath control, regulated by the mental repetition of AUM which balances *puraka* (breathing in), *recaka* (breathing out) and *kumbhaka* (retention of air in the lungs) so that they occupy equal lengths of time. By making his respiration progressively slower, until the rhythm of sleep is reached, the yogi lucidly 'penetrates' the dream state without losing full consciousness.

The example of Milarepa, one of the founders in the twelfth century of the Kargyupta school of Tibetan Buddhism, illustrates the difficulties and rewards of attempting to achieve conscious dreaming. Milarepa's biographer, Rechung, records that after eight years of study and instruction under his guru Marpa, he dreamt of his family home in ruins, and prepared to leave: 'My teacher set himself to prepare the mandala diagram. . . . Then he conferred upon me the last and highest initiations and the Mysteries of the Dream Symbols, and the Tantras whispered in the ear of the disciple by the guru.' After years of hardship and travel, Milarepa was still unable to reach even the first level of the Six Doctrines given him by Marpa. The *Chos-drug*, or Six Doctrines, is a Tibetan yogic text which lists the steps on the path to knowledge: 1) Vital Warmth, the driving force needed to begin the way of spiritual development; 2) Illusory Body, a teaching by which the yogi realizes that his body and all other objects in nature are illusory; 3) Dreams, a doctrine by which the yogi realizes that even as dreams are illusory, so are all *sangsaric* experiences in the waking state and in the dreaming state equally; 4) Clear Light; 5) *Bardo* or Intermediate State; 6) Transference.

Unable to generate Vital Warmth, Milarepa undertook eight years of meditation and purification in solitude in the Dragkar-Taso Cave, eating barely enough to keep alive. At the end of this period of isolation, he had reached the third level of the *Chos-drug*:

'By night, in my dreams, I could traverse the summit of Mt. Meru to its base – and I saw everything clearly as I went. Likewise in my dreams I could multiply myself into hundreds of personalities, all endowed with the same powers as myself. Each of my multiplied forms could traverse space and go to some Buddha Heaven, listen to the teachings there, and then come back and teach the *Dharma* to many persons. I could also transform my physical body into a mass of blazing fire, or into an expanse of flowing or calm water. Seeing that I had obtained infinite phenomenal powers even though it be but in my dreams, I was filled with happiness and encouragement.'

The yogi who realizes the teachings of the Dream Doctrine, penetrates the state of dreaming, and becomes active and creative in the realm of *taijasa*, has begun to grasp the illusion and to solve the problem of reality. When he goes to sleep, 'he takes along the material of this all-containing world, himself tears it apart, himself builds it up, and dreams by his own brightness, by his own light. Then this person becomes self-illumin-ated. There are no chariots there, no bridges, no roads, but he projects from himself chariots, bridges, roads. There are no tanks there, no lotus ponds, no streams. But he projects from himself tanks, lotus ponds, streams. For he is a creator . . . a god.'

PSYCHOANALYTIC TRADITIONS

Before 1899, when Sigmund Freud published his monumental study, *The Interpretation of Dreams*, European research into dreaming had been carried on by isolated individuals like Alfred Maury, who experimented with the effect of physical sense impressions on the dream – his example of the bed rail falling on his neck which 'caused' him to dream of being guillotined is well known – and Hervey de Saint-Denis, who over a period of twenty years sought to 'master the illusion of dreams' by controlling them with his conscious mind.

Medicine, at the time, was not interested in dreams, which were usually held to be meaningless hallucinations. It was against this medical background that Freud reacted. By studying his own dreams in detail, he evolved a theory of dreaming by which he understood dreams as the *disguised* fulfilment of the dreamer's infantile sexual needs. As most dreams were not overtly sexual, he maintained that the manifest dream, the dream which one recalls, has already been censored by the mind, and that behind it is a 'latent' dream to which it bears little resemblance. The 'manifest' dream needed to be disguised,

Freud thought, so that its content would not shock the dreamer into waking: 'Dreams are the guardians of sleep and not its disturbers.'

The four ways in which the latent dream content is disguised were categorized by Freud as condensation, displacement, secondary revision and symbolism, and he called these four processes 'the dream work'. Condensation is the mechanism by which several latent dream ideas are condensed into a single image in the manifest dream; for example, one's father, employer and analyst may be combined. By displacement, the emotion really connected with one situation may be attached to a very different one in order to distract the dreamer's attention from the actual object of his feelings. Secondary revision is the unconscious altering of the manifest dream as it is recalled, in an attempt to make sense of it. Although Freud pointed out that 'there are countless dreams which satisfy needs other than sexual', it was mainly the symbolization of sexual organs and activities that concerned him. In his patients' dreams he believed that he found a phallic symbolism in such images as knives, bananas, trees and spires, and symbols for the female genitals in images like pockets, holes and gates.

Freud's contribution to the study of dreaming rescued the subject from the periphery, and restored it to the centre of western man's concern. That he was able to do this in the climate of opinion prevailing at the turn of the century was extraordinary. Freud's approach to neurosis through the dream was so radical at the time that it was treated with contempt and dismissed as a mixture of obscenity and obscurity, and even C. G. Jung, by his own admission, was unable to appreciate its importance for a number of years. Freud provided the impetus for the twentieth century to explore the dream. André Breton paid him this eloquent tribute: 'Under the pretence of civilization and progress, we have managed to banish from the mind everything that may rightly or wrongly be termed superstition, or fancy; forbidden is any kind of search for truth which is not in accordance with accepted practices. It was, apparently, by pure chance that a part of our mental world which we pretended not to be concerned with any longer – and, in my opinion, by far the most important part – has been brought back to light. For this we must give thanks to the discoveries of Sigmund Freud. On the basis of these discoveries, a current of opinion is finally forming by means of which the human explorer will be able to carry his investigations much further.'

While Freud looked on the dream itself as a disturbed form of mental activity through which he could approach his patients' neuroses, C. G. Jung saw the dream as a normal, spontaneous and creative expression of the unconscious. Jung was the human explorer anticipated by Breton. He had been a younger colleague of Freud, and was considered by Freud as his 'heir apparent', but in 1914 Jung's disagreement with a number of Freud's theories, and with his overall approach, caused him to break away and follow his own understanding of the processes of the unconscious and the role of dreams.

Although Jung accepted certain basic principles of Freud's dream theory, such as condensation and symbolism, he rejected the 'disguise' theory completely: 'There is no reason under the sun why we should assume that the dream is a crafty device to lead us astray.' (H. G. Baynes has described Freud's disguise theory succinctly by suggesting that it is like the experience of an English visitor to Paris who assumes that Parisians are talking nonsense in order to make a fool of him.) Jung was unconvinced, too, by the emphasis that Freud placed on wish-fulfilment and by what seemed to him to be Freud's over-valuation of the sexual aspect of the unconscious: 'There was no mistaking the fact that Freud was emotionally involved in his sexual theory to an extraordinary degree. When he spoke of it, his tone became urgent, almost anxious. . . . I had a strong feeling that for him sexuality was a sort of numinosum. . . . I can still recall how vividly Freud said to me, "My dear Jung, promise me never to abandon the sexual theory. That is the most essential thing of all. You see, we must make a dogma of it, an unshakable bulwark." In some astonishment I asked him, "A bulwark – against what?" To which he replied, "Against the black tide of mud," and here he hesitated for a moment, then added – "of occultism."'

But above all, Jung was unable to accept the reductionism of Freudian theory, by which the individuality of any one of a class of symbols was reduced to a single idea. Such a system denies the uniqueness of particular symbols, and Jung replaced it with a method of amplification, of extending the significance of a particular dream image with elements taken from mythological and ethnological parallels.

The openness of Jung's approach allowed him, as June Singer says, 'to let his speculations run free as he entered the realm of the mysterious, without attempting to concretize the ineffable experience'. Within his own dreams and the dreams of his patients, he discovered certain archetypes which he described as 'the numinous structural elements of the psyche which possess a certain autonomy and specific energy which enables them to attract, out of the conscious mind, those contents which are best suited to themselves. . . . It was manifestly not a question of inherited ideas, but of an inborn disposition to produce parallel images, or rather of identical psychic structures common to all men, which I later called the archetypes of the collective unconscious. . . . These archetypes do not represent anything external, non-psychic, although they do, of course, owe the concreteness of their imagery to impressions received from without. Rather, independently of, and sometimes in direct contrast to, the outward forms they may take, they represent the life and essence of a non-individual psyche.'

Freud's system of analysis could at best obtain for the individual a clear present that reflected adjustment to the past, by releasing the repressed feelings in a moment of catharsis, so transcending the totally negative neurosis. But the method is – in the sense that it is concerned with removing past ills – essentially backward-looking. Jung developed a finalistic attitude which valued even the neurosis as part of the psychic life that is trying to advance. 'All psychological phenomena have some sense of purpose in them,' Jung wrote. The dream has as its purpose the drive towards individuation: the discovery of the self.

The creative dreamer

When we dream, we can learn to bring back something of value to society. The creative dreamer does not return empty-handed. He or she is an explorer of the dream world, returning with a song, a dance, a cure, with information about the future, information about a distant place or with a new idea of some kind.

The validation of the song is that it is effective. The dance is good; the cure works; the prophecy is true; the telepathic experience is confirmed; and the idea makes sense. F. A. Kekulé, the German chemist, wrote about a dream that came to his aid: 'I turned the chair to the fireplace and sank into a half-sleep. The atoms flitted before my eyes . . . wriggling and turning like snakes. And see, what was that? One of the snakes seized its own tail and the image whirled scornfully before my eyes. As though from a flash of lightening I awoke. I occupied the rest of the night in working out the consequences of the hypothesis.' The consequences were the discovery of the formula for benzene. 'Learn to dream, gentlemen,' he advised a scientific convention in 1890.

Creative dreaming is universal. There is a continuity of so-called 'paranormal' experience in relationship to dreams that extends from supposedly primitive peoples like the Pygmies, whose well-documented prophetic clairvoyance in sleep is mentioned by Mircea Eliade, to modern areligious societies. 'He giveth unto his beloved in their sleep', according to Psalm 127.

The act of receiving, whether the gift is a song or pre-cognitive information, is the essential mark of a creative dream, a term describing both 'paranormal' dream experiences like precognition, dream telepathy and clairvoyance, and songs, dances and ideas inspired in or by the dream. Separating the 'paranormal' from the 'normal' is a sign of modern man's discontinuity of experience, for the term 'paranormal' has no organic meaning: it is defined only by negation, by the withdrawal of successive material causes for an event until only the 'impossible', the 'paranormal', remains.

Within Islam, for example, the continuity and integration of the numinous dream experience with the 'normality' of material life has remained intact. The institution of the *ad'han*, the call to prayer, was received in a dream. At the time, the Prophet was eager to introduce a recognizable call to prayer for the faithful, just as the Jews were called to the synagogue with the trumpet, and the early Christians summoned to church by the sound of the rattle. During prayers, one of Mohammed's followers, Abdullah ben Zayd, fell asleep, and dreamed of a man dressed in green who was carrying a rattle. He asked if he could buy the rattle to use as a call to prayer, but the man in green said to him: 'Call out, "There is no god but God and Mohammed is his Prophet."' As soon as he awoke, Abdullah ben Zayd told the Prophet of his dream, and Mohammed instructed him to teach the exact phrase that he had heard to Bilal, who became the first muezzin.

Kilton Stewart records a Senoi dream-inspired dance which enabled the dreamer, like St Peter, to introduce a cultural change without parallel in his own society:

'Datu Bintung . . . had a dream which succeeded in breaking down the major social barriers in clothing and food habits between the Senoi and the surrounding Chinese and Mohammedan colonies. Only those who performed the dance he had received in his dream were required to change their food habits and wear the new clothing, but the dance was so good that nearly all the Senoi along the border chose to do it. . . . Another feature of the dream involved the ceremonial status of women, making them more nearly the equals of men. . . . This was a pure creative action of the dream, for which there were no models in the surrounding cultures.'

Among the Teton Sioux, Papago and Chippewa, as with almost all American Indian groups, the song/poem is not a work of art. Almost always the result of a dream, the song is, as Kenneth Rexroth says, 'holy, . . . an object of supernatural awe, and as such, an important instrument in the control of reality on the highest place':

(1) *where*
the wind
is blowing
the wind
is roaring
I stand
westward
the wind
is blowing
the wind
is roaring
I stand

(2) *owls*
(were) hooting
in the passing of the night
owls
(were) hooting

(3) *where the mountain crosses*
on top of the mountain
I do not myself know where
I wandered where my mind and heart
seemed to be lost
I wandered away

(4) *(the deer's song)*
my shining horns

The first song was given by wolves to a Teton Sioux, Brave Buffalo, in a dream; the second, by an elk, to another Teton Sioux, Teal Duck; the third, in a dream, to a Papago woman whose name was not recorded, and the fourth to a Chippewa, Meckawigabau, in a dream in which he became a buffalo and was given these words by other buffalo. If the words of these dream songs are sometimes cryptic, and their meanings obscure, it is because their esoteric significance is concealed from the uninitiated. Another Papago woman commented: 'The song is very short because we know so much.' The songs are at one and the same time the words brought back verbatim from the dream encounter with the divinity, and the path by which the singer can return: an instrument for recreating the numinous experience.

Sometimes the dream or vision in which the dreamer receives a song is spontaneous, and sometimes induced; but it is always supported by the structure of the society which allows it to happen. Even in the west, there is a saying that 'Inspiration comes in dreams', and Kekulé and others, of course, have taken this possibility seriously.

Deliberately induced dreaming is of two kinds: dreams induced by prayer, fasting or drugs; and incubation, in which the power to induce the dream lies not in the individual's heightened awareness, but in a place which has potent magical qualities. Personally induced dreams, like Papago Foot's, may also occur at a magical or incubation site, but the inducing of the 'god within' always takes precedence over the holy ground.

The cult of Aesculapius, or Asklepios, was the most highly organized and widespread incubation cult in the ancient world. By the second century there were more than 300 active temples throughout Greece and Rome, devoted to curing by the intervention of the archetypal healer who appeared in dreams to the pilgrims at his shrines. As in the American Indian vision quest, the deity was approached only after rigorous fasting and purification. An inscription at the entrance to the temple at Epidaurus read: 'He who enters the temple perfumed with incense must be pure, and purity is to have only pious feelings.' After sacrifices of an ox, sheep or wheat cakes, oil and incense, and an evening of ecstatic prayer to the god to grant them the dream that they desired, the pilgrims slept on the skins of the sacrificial animals amidst the harmless yellow snakes of the region; for the serpent was the living symbol of the god. Originally, in the temple of Epidaurus, the god appeared to the invalid in a dream which was itself a miraculous cure; later, in Rome, the dream was no longer a cure, but a means of receiving divine medical advice.

Knowledge of these later practices comes from the *Sacred Orations* of Aristides (AD 150), in which he described his cure after a long illness. In his dreams he was given commandments: to go barefoot in winter; to use emetics; even, to sacrifice one of his fingers. He movingly described the intensity of his experience: 'One listened and heard things, sometimes in a dream, sometimes in waking life. One's hair stood on end; one cried and felt happy; one's heart swelled out but not with vainglory. What human being could put this experience into words? But anyone who has been through it will share my knowledge and recognize the state of my mind.'

Incubation is meeting the god half-way: the human rises and the divine descends. In these incubation rites the dreamer is no longer seeking a creation, a song, but a healing, a re-creation of what he or she sees as original health. It is not a search for 'power' in don Juan's meaning of the word, not a spiritual way, but a material desire on the part of the pilgrim. In incubation, the creative dream is not the invalid's, but God's.

In dream telepathy, pre-cognition and prophecy, the 'song' that the dreamer receives is a specific piece of information about something taking place somewhere else, or something that will occur sometime in the future. In the first case, the material concept of space is disrupted, and in the second, the idea of time as a linear progression from past to future is destroyed.

Although dream telepathy is reported to have been practised with great precision by some Sufi groups at the time of the Ottoman Empire, modern examples of spontaneous experiences of this kind, while clearly showing a telepathic effect, are usually perceived either partially or unclearly. A dream of C. G. Jung's is an example of this type:

'I dreamed that my wife's bed was in a deep pit with stone walls. It was a grave and somehow had a suggestion of classical antiquity about it. Then I heard a deep sigh, as if someone was giving up the ghost. A figure that resembled my wife sat up in the pit and floated upwards. It wore a white gown into which curious black symbols were woven. I awoke, roused my wife, and checked the time. It was three o'clock in the morning. The dream was so curious that I thought at once that it might signify a death. At seven o'clock came the news that a cousin of my wife's had died at three o'clock that morning.'

These dreams, in which the telepathic content – in this case, the idea of death and the precise timing – is interwoven with a complex of symbols that are vividly related to the dream content but only peripherally to the waking reality to which the telepathy relates, are probably unclear because the dreamer is 'unawakened'. Conscious or 'awakened' versions of these dreams will be discussed later.

Recent controlled experiments in dream telepathy, like those of Drs Montague Ullman and Stanley Krippner at the Maimonides Dream Laboratory in New York, have succeeded in validating the reality of dream telepathy. In their experiments, the subjects are attached to electroencephalographs which record their brain wave patterns (EEG), and to electro-oculographs which record their rapid eye movements (REM). With the onset of dreaming, which is noted by REM activity, and by a recognizable EEG pattern, an experimenter in a distant room tries to 'project' a randomly selected target picture or image into the subject's dream. Before their period of dreaming ends, the subjects are awakened and asked to recall their dreams. Successful as these experiments have been in establishing – in 'rational', scientific terms – that dream telepathy is not, as Aristotle suggested, merely an example of coincidence, they have made little progress towards evolving a theory of how it works.

One rather precise explanation of the workings of telepathic and pre-cognitive dreams was suggested by J. W. Dunne in his book *An Experiment with Time*. Dunne argued that such phenomena are not paranormal, but that all dreams contain information concerning both past and future events. The reason why precognition is not reported daily is, of course, that most dreams are not recalled, and that even when a pre-cognitive dream incident is remembered, it is automatically dismissed by the waking mind as impossible. The exceptions are dreams that are so significant to the dreamer that the waking mind cannot reject them, which is why so many spontaneous telepathic and pre-cognitive dreams concern a close relative or friend of the dreamer, as in Jung's dream. To allow for the atemporal perspective from which the future, as well as the past, can be seen, Dunne postulated a series of Selves, each of whose consciousness was dimensionally superior to its predecessor's. Thus, while solving what seems to be a problem in definition for our materialist culture, Dunne's theory created the further problem of infinite regression.

Dunne suggested that minor events foreseen in dreams would occur within a few days, but no method has yet been devised to subject prophecy to such rigorous experimental techniques as those devised by Ullman and Krippner to test dream telepathy. In prophetic traditions like the biblical, the only validation of prophetic dreams was that they came true, and the only method of seeing if they came true was to wait. Estimating the length of time it may be necessary to wait is difficult even for prophets.

Perhaps the greatest American Indian seer was Black Elk. It is usual to view him as a supremely tragic figure, a man of moving intensity whose great prophetic vision seemed to remain unfulfilled. The central message of his vision was that the Sioux nation, which had been broken and scattered by some of the worst Indian-white confrontations in American history, could be made whole again through faith and correct ritual.

Having failed to save his people with a literal enactment of his vision, Black Elk moves the problem of his vision's fulfilment onto a transcendent plane – for the transcendent is real in a way that history is not – and recognizing that the essential success or failure of his prophecy will not take place on the material historical plane, he delivers the record of his vision to his conquerors in a highly potent, recharged form.

The repetition of the complex sequences of his vision as he dictated it to John Neihardt – once in telling of the experience and once in describing the ceremonies based on it – is an example of the kind of magical repetition used by Brave Buffalo in the text quoted earlier, and a major formal pattern in most dream songs, for repetition means accumulation of power. Black Elk stated that Neihardt had been chosen (as don Juan chose Castaneda) to be his pupil, and to pass on his special knowledge to all mankind. Nor is there any doubt that Black Elk intended his 'autobiography' itself to be a powerful, coercive, numinous means of transmitting the Word he had received to the 'enemies' of his people. As a man who has received the Word, he is able to manipulate reality through words, and he begins his narrative by saying that the story of his life is 'the story of a mighty vision given to a man too weak to use it: of a holy tree that should have flourished in a people's heart with flowers and singing birds, and now is withered; and of a people's dream that died in bloody snow. But if this vision was true and mighty as I know, *it is true and mighty yet*; for such things are of the spirit, and it is only in the darkness of their eyes that men get lost.'

Black Elk's prophetic vision, originally for the Sioux, is redirected to the readers of his autobiography. He has succeeded in transmitting the message, and the prophecy is, perhaps, yet to be fulfilled.

The awakened dreamer

When Milarepa left his cave after eight years of meditation, he was able to dream consciously. He was able to create the forms within his dreams: 'I could . . . transform my body into a blazing mass of fire, or into an expanse of calm or flowing water.' He was able to project himself freely outside his physical body: 'I could travel the universe in every direction unimpededly.' Milarepa was in the process of becoming a god, the conscious being who creates the world.

What does it mean, to be conscious in a dream, to be aware and in control during sleep? It is an experience that makes *non*-sense of a materialistic world-view, because it is in direct opposition to its definitions: 'Having some conscious experience or other, no matter what, is not what is meant by being asleep', a contemporary positivist philosopher has asserted. The esoteric traditions on this point can perhaps be summarized in Gurdjieff's statement that most men are asleep when they think they are awake. To wake in dreams is one way to begin to awake from the dream of life; to wake up to the realization that, like the figures one can consciously create in dreams, the dreamer is dreamed too. This mystery was expressed concisely by the ancient Egyptians, whose word for dream derived from the verb 'to awaken'.

Lucidity is the first step of the awakened dreamer:

'"I am going to teach you right here the first step to power", don Juan said, "I am going to teach you how to *set up dreaming*!"

'He looked at me and again asked me if I knew what he meant. I did not. I was hardly following him at all. He explained that to "set up dreaming" meant to have a concise and pragmatic control over the general situation of a dream, comparable to the control one has over any choice in the desert, such as climbing up a hill or remaining in the shade of a water canyon.

'"You must start by doing something very simple," he said. "Tonight in your dreams you must look at your hands."'

Choosing to be aware of a particular object and to sustain the awareness through the dream state is one of the most common ways to achieve lucidity. Frederick Van Eeden, an early psychotherapist, first achieved consciousness in his dreams by observing a detail: 'I dreamt that I was floating through a landscape with bare trees . . . and that I remarked that the perspective of the branches and twigs changed quite naturally. Then I made the reflection, during sleep, that my fancy would never be able to invent . . . an image as intricate as the perspective movement . . . seen in floating by.' It is not noticing the similarity to waking life that triggers lucidity, but an awareness, which can come either from noticing that the dream image is too like the waking image to have been invented, or that one must be dreaming because the image is too unlike the waking image. '"Dreaming is real when one has succeeded in bringing everything into focus. . . . You don't have to look at your hands," don Juan said. "Like I've said, pick anything at all. But pick one thing in advance and find it in your dreams."'

In India, the specific yogic technique for obtaining continuity of consciousness while entering the dream state is awareness and control of breath, *pranayama*. As a focus of concentration, breath, being immaterial, is less likely to lead the novice from the material world into a world in which the dream forms and images seem to constitute a second, but imitation, material world. In some Tibetan yogic schools, the objects of concentration are the images of a divinity in terrible or awesome form, violent enough to shock the novice into lucidity when he recognizes the image in a dream. Because certain sects of this left-handed path of Tantra have tended to concentrate on the illusory 'reality' of the demonic image, rather than on the more abstract process of observing the *puraka* (breathing in), *recaka* (breathing out), and *kumbhaka* (retention of air in the lungs), they have been accused of merely substituting one form of materialism for another.

One must ultimately transcend the dream state, but one must first experience fully its specific, immaterial form of reality, and learn the laws which govern conscious action there. While Jung, too, specifically warned of the dangers of hypostatizing the forms encountered in the realm of what he called 'psychic reality', his conclusions on this point involve a profound paradox: 'Instead of allowing himself to be convinced that the demon is an illusion, he [everyone] ought to experience once more the reality of this illusion. He should learn to acknowledge these psychic forces anew . . . his dissociative tendencies are actual psychic personalities possessing a differential reality. They are real when they are not recognized as real, and unconsciously projected; they are relatively real when they are brought into relationship with consciousness (in religious terms, when a cult exists); but they are unreal to the extent that consciousness detaches itself from its contents. This last stage, however, is reached only when life has been lived so exhaustively and with such devotion that no obligations remain unfulfilled. . . . It is futile to lie to ourselves about this. Wherever we are still attached we are still possessed.'

While one may need the fearful shocks of recognition to achieve lucidity in dreams – as the Senoi are able to turn dreams of falling into dreams of flying, and the demonic figures encountered by Eskimo and Lapp shamans serve the purpose of startling the dreamer into conscious awareness – one must not be trapped by the apparently authentic illusions of the dream world.

' "Ordinary dreams get very vivid as soon as you begin to set up dreaming," don Juan said. "That vividness and clarity is a formidable barrier." '

' "The next step in *setting up dreaming* is to learn to travel. . . . The same way you have learned to look at your hands you can will yourself to move, to go places. First you have to establish a place you want to go to . . . then will yourself to go there." '

Travelling, flying or astral projection and journeys out-of-the-body, as these experiences are often described in the west, are universal modes of existence in conscious dreams. When, according to the various terminologies employed, the Self, the soul, the warrior, the astral body, the hunter, the *Bardo*-body, the Knower, becomes capable of perceiving a reality apart from the material reality of objects, this aspect of the dreamer can learn to move freely through space and time in a world which is distinct from the image of the physical world, although interpenetrated with it.

When awakened dreamers begin to explore this non-material world, they often find themselves bathed in a bright light. At first, this light appears to be coloured, but after a long period of spiritual development, the dreamer's perception alters to an experience of pure white light. A dream of the Sufi Shamsoddin Lahiji contains one of his early experiences of cosmic light, as well as his first dreamed experience of flying:

'I saw that the entire universe, in the structure it presents, consists of light. Everything had become one colour. . . . I wanted to fly in the air, but I saw that there was something resembling a piece of wood at my feet which prevented me from taking flight. With violent emotion, I kicked the ground in every possible manner until this piece of wood let go. Like an arrow shooting forth from the bow . . . I rose and moved into the distance.'

In the context of cultures like the Tibetan, Islamic, Senoi, or Maricopa, an esoteric or exoteric structure exists to provide the novice dreamer with sufficient information to make sense of experiences in the dream state; if not a clear map, at least a plan of action. But it may happen that a dreamer, without any previous unusual dream experiences, and without instruction from a teacher, is plunged spontaneously into conscious dreams, travelling and the experience of light. Sometimes when this occurs, the dreamer chooses to remain at the level of simple lucidity, and spends the dream time forever testing the apparent reality and non-material composition of this world, as Frederick Van Eeden did, by striking wine glasses to see if they would break in dreams as they would in waking life.

In other cases, the dreamer proceeds to explore the dream world alone and without help.

Robert Monroe is an American businessman who began having spontaneous out-of-the-body experiences in 1958. The experiences terrified him, but after convincing himself that he was not insane and that the state was in some sense real, he developed his own method of entering the dream world consciously. He projected to specific locations, collecting evidence to prove to himself that he had 'really' been there, even on one occasion pinching a friend who was awake, to prove that he was present. Monroe experienced projection either as a form of flying, as if physically, or at times there was simply the sensation of 'movement through a light blurred area'. He experienced the light phenomenon as an almost tangible, impersonal beam of light of enormous power that entered and transfixed him; and he has recounted his battles with the dream forms who attacked him:

'I remembered the visualized thought of fire, and that it hadn't seemed much use, but had helped a little. This time, I tried thinking of electricity. I visualized two pieces of highly charged wire. I mentally stuck them into the side of that part of the entity that I had pulled off my back. Immediately the mass deflated, went limp, and seemed to die. As it did, a bat-like thing squeaked past my head and went out of the window. I felt that I had won.'

Like the Tibetans, whose grotesque and terrifying visions he spontaneously shared, Monroe recognized that this dream world is real – or at least as real as the waking world – but its physical forms appear to be plastic and alterable at will:

'The Second Body [Monroe's term for the active participant in conscious dream experience] is very plastic and may take whatever form is suitable to or desired by the individual. The ability to 'stretch out' the arm to three times its normal length points to such elasticity. . . . If no special form is transmitted by the mind or will at a given moment . . . the familiar humanoid shape is maintained through some automatic thought-habituality.'

There is a second kind of awakened dreaming which the American psychologist Charles Tart refers to as the 'high dream'. The high dream is 'an experience occurring during sleep in which you find yourself in another world, the dream world, *and* in which you recognize *during* the dream that you are in an altered state of consciousness'. An altered state of consciousness or ASC is any mode of consciousness other than that normally experienced during the waking state. In Tart's definition of the high dream, the altered state is one which is similar to, but not necessarily identical with, the high induced by a chemical psychedelic:

'I dreamed I got high on some sort of gaseous substance, like LSD in gas form. Space took on an expanded, high quality, my body (dream body) was filled with a delicious sensation of warmth, my mind "high" in an obvious but indescribable way. It only lasted a minute and then I was awakened by one of the kids calling out and my wife getting up to see what was the matter. Then the most amazing thing happened; I stayed high even though awake! . . . the expanded and warm quality of time and space carried over into my perception of the room. It stayed this way for a couple of minutes, amazing me at the time because I was clearly high, as well as recalling my high dream.'

The concept of the high dream could easily be extended to include other ASC experiences such as meditation or ecstatic states. It is particularly interesting that the high state can be carried over into waking life, which suggests that the ecstatic ASC, like the Sufic *alam al-mithral*, is located in an ontological area that can be approached either from another ASC, such as the dream state, or from the waking condition. A similar experience is related in the following dream account, although in this case the ASC referred to is *latihan*, an exercise of the inner faculties which Claudio Naranjo describes as 'expressive meditation':

'I was having an unpleasant dream in which I was confronted with what seemed like an insurmountable problem. Suddenly, I realized that I might be able to solve the problem if I did a *latihan*. I closed my eyes for a minute, "received", and entered the state. As the force moved me, I experienced and recognized "my own" *latihan*, by which I mean that what was happening to me was a continuation of what had been happening to me in waking *latihans* around this time. And as I realized this, I gradually became fully lucid, in the dream. I realized that I had entered the *latihan* while dreaming, and that I knew it. But at that point, I woke up, still in a state of *latihan* that continued for several minutes.'

In this dream, in addition to the criteria specified by Tart, the dreamer apparently achieved lucidity in the ASC while aware that he was dreaming.

The most complete contemporary theory of the dream state in relationship to conscious dreaming is that taught by Bhagwan Shree Rajneesh, whose work integrates many aspects of both Hindu and Muslim esoteric traditions. According to this teaching, we have seven bodies – the physical, etheric, astral, mental, spiritual, cosmic and Nirvanic – each capable of dreaming its own kind of dreams, in its own dimensions, according to its own laws. The closer a dream approaches to the Nirvanic level, the less it is composed of fantasy which is a personal projection of the dreamer, and the closer it comes to reality, authenticity, or to the essential dream quality which is 'something which is not in existence'.

However, to merely experience these seven bodies and their seven different kinds of dreaming may actually be a hindrance to *apprehending* the seven levels of reality, although the dreamer might be able to dream prophetic dreams, to experience astral projection or to have telepathic experiences. To truly know each of the seven realities, one must become conscious in each of the seven kinds of dreams. One must learn to be an awakened dreamer on each of the seven levels.

'The physical body creates its own dream. If your stomach is upset then a particular type of dream is created.' This is the kind of dream that Maury experimented with. It also includes, according to Rajneesh, Freud's concept of the wish-fulfilling dream: 'If you have suppressed sex, then there is every possibility of sexual fantasies.' At this level, the dream is nothing but fantasy; it is totally unreal: 'Sometimes in the ordinary dream, there may be a part of the etheric or a part of the astral; then the dream becomes a muddle . . . then you cannot understand it; because your seven bodies are simultaneously in existence, and something from one realm can pass the barrier of another.'

The 'etheric body' can travel in space, and when this travelling is unconscious, it is remembered as a dream. Out-of-the-body experiences of the sort that Monroe experimented with when he visited friends in his dreams are conscious experiences of the etheric body and can be induced by *japa* (repetition of mantras), by the use of perfumes as understood by some Sufi groups or by meditation on certain colours.

'The astral mind can go into the past, into the whole infinite series of pasts from amoeba to man. This astral mind has been interpreted in Jung's psychology as the collective unconscious.' To experience this dream state consciously one must enter it without preconceptions concerning the soul: 'If the astral dreaming is a dream and not real, then you will be crippled by the fear of death. The fear of death – that is the touchstone.' To overcome the fear of death in the dream experience, not by faith that the soul is immortal, but through knowledge, is the way to achieve consciousness at this level. This is the level at which the Senoi live in dreams.

The 'mental body' can travel into the past and into the future as it relates to the dreamer or to those close to him. The images in these dreams are usually clear. Conscious mental body dreams can be induced by long periods of fasting and isolation, and by rites such as the Muslim *istiq'ara*. This is the stage that Milarepa had reached when he left the cave of Dragkar-Taso after eight years of Tantric meditation. All the arts originate in this fourth type of dream; a person who can dream in the fourth realm can become a great artist, but this may be a barrier to true knowledge. Rajneesh warns that 'One should not create anything, otherwise it will be created. . . . One must be constantly aware that there is no wish, no imagination, no image, no God, no guru – otherwise they will all be created out of you. You will be the creator. And they are so . . . blissful that one longs to create them. This is the last barrier for the seeker; if one crosses this then he will not face another barrier greater than this.' As long as the dreamer creates an image, he will go on dreaming, for only 'the witnessing mind is the path toward the real'.

'The fifth body, the spiritual, crosses the realm of the individual; it crosses the realm of time. Now you are in eternity.' This is the level on which all the great myths were dreamed, the myth of the flood, the myth of creation. 'Two persons who have realized the fifth body can dream simultaneously.' In spiritual consciousness there is no distinction between dream and reality; there is only a difference, as between a figure and its reflection in the mirror. In the spiritual dream, the dream is in the mirror.

On the sixth level of being, from the cosmic body, come dreams of pure Existence: 'So those who have dreamed into the Cosmic dimensions have been creators of the great systems . . . the theories of Brahma and Maya, theories of Oneness, theories of the Infinite. But although far beyond the individual, beyond categories of time and space, on this level there is still a desire to cling to existence, a fear of non-existence. Matter and the mind have become one, but not Existence and Non-Existence, not Being and Non-Being. They are still separate.'

And the seventh body, the Nirvanic, 'has its own dreams, dreams of Non-Existence, dreams of Nothingness. . . . The "yes" has been left behind, and even the "no" is not a "no". . . . Now the FORMLESS IS. Now there is no sound but the soundless. "NOW" IS THIS SILENCE. The dreams of silence are total, unending.'

1 The dream mediates between the worlds of matter and spirit, time and eternity. In Jacob's dream the ladder with angels ascending and descending it symbolizes the ease of transition between these levels of reality in the mind of the dreamer. Time is abolished, and analogous incidents of past and future are perceived simultaneously as the dream opens the way from one world to another, establishing a relationship between mundane and spiritual realities. (Jacob's Dream, from the Lambeth Bible, England, 12th c.)

invenies vidre abjaham et ihce ma   nibre filiu rio alno stuphete

BETHEL · VBI · VHRISTI   LAPIDE

WAS · DEVS

2, 3 In sleep, when the barriers established by the ego are lowered, the dreamer's perception may extend beyond the rational boundaries of the conscious self. Bes (left), the Egyptian god of roads and ways, was invoked for protection against the powers of the unknown that might overwhelm the dreamer as nightmares. Images of the god were carved on the wooden headrests the Egyptians used as pillows. Shown here in fourfold form and wielding a sword, Bes personified forces beyond consciousness while at the same time guarding the threshold between consciousness and the unknown in dreams.

Hypnos (above), the Greek god of sleep, was the twin brother of Death and the son of Night, herself the daughter of Chaos. Only a generation removed from the dark origins of the psyche, Sleep and his brothers, the People of Dreams, inhabited a realm at the outer limits of the real world, close to the anti-world of non-existence. (2 Bes, limestone relief, Egypt, 3rd–1st c. BC; 3 Hypnos, head of lost bronze statue after Greek original of 4th c. BC.)

4, 5 For centuries the philosophical traditions of India have understood dreaming as an integral part of the layered structure of the psychic and spiritual universe, and as a potential area of consciousness, where the 'illusion of reality' can be experienced and perceived.

The essential mantra AUM (OM) (left) is a model for understanding the four levels of consciousness: the waking state, dreaming, dreamless sleep and the indescribable state which encompasses and transcends the first three. Separately, the letters A, U, M evoke the first three levels; their totality, AUM, combines and transcends them in the fourth.

Unfortunately, the significance of the esoteric theories diagrammed so
precisely by the Chumash Indians of California will now never be fully
understood, but it is known that attempts to penetrate the dreaming and
waking states with equal lucidity were made by the Chumash shamans,
who formalized the 'journeys' of their souls in these mandalas (right).
(4 Om, gouache on cloth, India, 18th c.; 5 Chumash cave painting,
California, USA, copy by Campbell Grant.)

6, 7 The idea of the dream as a
source of divine revelation has
resulted in cultural innovations
and has influenced historical
events. A dream of Abdullah ben
Zayd, one of the companions of
the prophet Mohammed, was
institutionalized in the *ad'han*, or
call to prayer (left), now heard
five times a day throughout the
Islamic world. The first muezzin,
Bilal, was taught to repeat the
words heard in the dream: 'There
is no god but God, and
Mohammed is His prophet.'

The future pharaoh Thotmosis
IV 'about the time of midday, had
stretched himself to rest in the
shade of the great god Hermakhis
[the Sphinx of Gizeh] when sleep
overtook him. He dreamt it in his
slumber at the moment when the
sun was at the zenith, and it
seemed to him as though the god
spoke to him with his own
mouth', commanding him to
repair the neglect to his temple by
clearing away the sand which had
accumulated over it. In return the
god promised him the throne of
Egypt. Thotmosis is twice
represented worshipping the god
on the plaque (right) he erected to
commemorate his dream and its
outcome. (6 Muezzin; 7 Great
Sphinx of Gizeh, Egypt,
c. 2620 BC.)

William Blake.

I suppose it to be a Vision

Indeed I remember a
conversation with M.ʳˢ Blake
about it.

Frederick Tatham

8, 9 'A spirit and a vision are not, as modern philosophy supposes, a cloudy vapour, or a nothing; they are organized and minutely articulated beyond all that mortal and perishing nature can produce. He who does not imagine in stronger and better lineaments, and in a stronger and better light than his perishing and mortal eye can see, does not imagine at all.' William Blake (left).

'In the year 1525 between Wednesday and Thursday after Whitsunday during the night I saw this appearance in my sleep, how many great waters fell from heaven. The first struck the earth about four miles away from me with a terrific force, with tremendous clamour and clash, drowning the whole land. I was so sore afraid that I awoke from it before the other waters fell. And the waters which had fallen were very abundant. Some of them fell further away, some nearer, and they all came down from such a great height that they all seemed to fall with equal slowness. But when the first water, which hit the earth, was almost approaching, it fell with such swiftness, wind and roaring, that I was so frightened when I awoke that my whole body trembled and for a long while I could not come to myself. So when I arose in the morning I painted above here as I had seen it. God turn all things to the best.' Albrecht Dürer (right). (8 Drawing by William Blake, England, early 19th c.; 9 Notebook page by Albrecht Dürer, Germany, 1525.)

10, 11 Kwan Hiu, painter, poet and monk, created a series of paintings of Buddhist saints seen in his dreams: 'Before painting one of these venerable personages, he prayed each time and obtained the figure in a dream. He retained it in his mind, and his portraits did not conform with accepted standards.' A Hall of the Arhats Seen in Dreams was erected in his honour to house the series. The Bodhisattva Samantabhadra (left) was not depicted according to contemporary conventions as an Indian prince, but disguised as a monk; the physical type of the Bodhisattva was considered a radical innovation in style.

the Portrait of a Man who instructed
Mr. Blake in Painting &c. in his Dreams

Imagination of a Man who Mr Blake has see.
instruction in Painting &c from

William Blake, painter, poet and visionary, insisted on the ontological
reality of his dreams and visions. The 'Man who instructed Mr Blake in
Painting in his Dreams', a 'friend in eternity' (right), was meticulously
drawn so that others, too, might begin to recognize aspects of this real
world. Blake declared it was his 'great task: to open the eternal worlds,
to open the immortal eyes of man inwards, into the world of thought,
into Eternity. . . .' (10 Detail of ink drawing by Kwan Hiu, China,
9th–10th c.; 11 Pencil drawing by William Blake, England, c. 1819, ?
copy by John Linnell.)

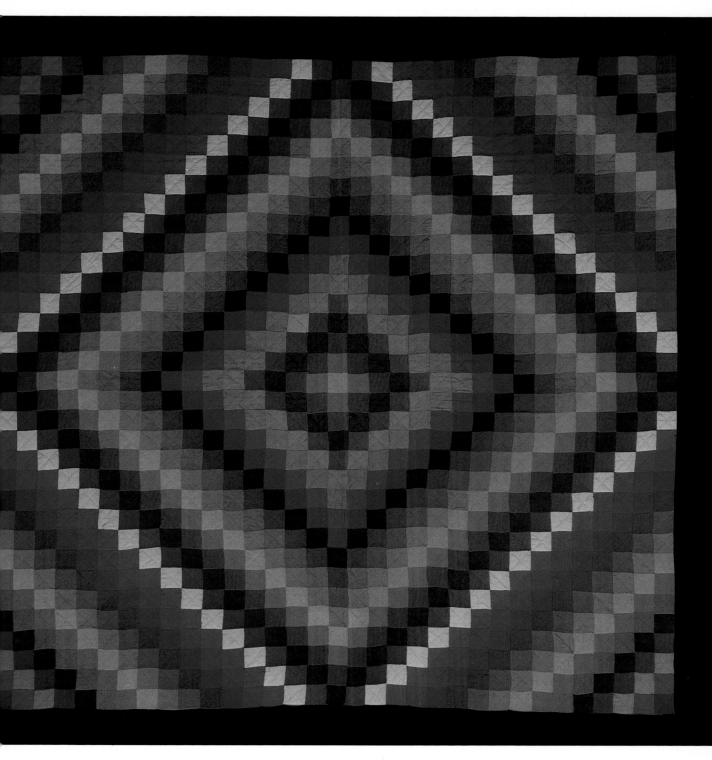

12, 13 The language that formalizes and manifests ecstatic and mystical dream experiences must always appear cryptic and personal. It serves as a mnemonic for recalling or recreating the original feeling of the experience. The Ghost Dance movement that preoccupied many American Indian tribes during the nineteenth century encouraged visionary experiences and the development of individual sensitivity to inner realities. Designs for ceremonial clothing were received in dreams or trance visions. On this Arapaho dress (left) the dreamer has represented herself standing between light and darkness under a crescent moon symbolizing the sensible world of changing phenomena. The turtle, symbol of material existence, is counterbalanced by birds representing elevation of spirit, transcendence and freedom. Stars symbolize aspects of the human spirit in its struggle against darkness.

The luminous aspects of mystical dream states are clearly communicated in a quilt appropriately titled 'Granny's Dream' (above), whose pattern expands from the central cross in a series of bands of vibrating colour. (12 Arapaho buckskin Ghost Dance costume, Oklahoma, USA, *c.* 1890; 13 Amish quilt made to traditional 19th-century design, USA.)

14,15 A formal recognition of the significance of the dream is the basis of certain tendencies in contemporary western art. Jean Arp (above) described his early reliefs as 'dreamed plastic works'. He wrote: 'Reason tells man to stand above nature and to be the measure of all things. Thus man thinks he is able to live and to create against the laws of nature and he creates aberrations. . . . Man should be like nature, without measure'; and 'A dreamer can make eggs as big as houses.'

André Masson (right) used a variety of methods to induce the ecstatic trance-like state in which much of his work was produced. As he worked he repeated aloud what were known as 'support words': attraction . . . transmutation . . . whirling; he also sang. The 'automatic' drawings and paintings produced in this way can be seen as representations of what passes through the mind in the absence of revision or conscious control. André Breton, the theoretician of Surrealism, described the process as 'a kind of psychic automatism, which corresponds very closely to a dream state'. (14 Winged Configuration, relief by Jean Arp, France, 1925; 15 The Portico, drawing by André Masson, France, 1925; see also pp. 88–89.)

andré Masson
1925

16, 17, 18 Few individuals in western society have attempted to explore the dream state consciously, accepting the reality of the immaterial. Hervey de Saint-Denis made detailed visual and verbal records of his experiences (below). He described hypnagogic visions (images seen in the state between waking and sleeping) as 'wheels of light, tiny revolving suns, coloured bubbles rising and falling . . . bright lines that cross and interlace, that roll up and make circles, lozenges and other geometric shapes'.

Ophiel, a contemporary occultist, has described the colours (right) 'you will see just before you break through into the Astral Plane with your newly developed clairvoyant inner sight. . . . The first thing to appear is the solid black. Then next the colours begin to appear through the black. . . . The black then thins out and away, the colours become more brilliant, and finally burst out into the blinding pure white Astral light.' (16 Frontispiece of *Les Rêves et les moyens de les diriger*, by the Marquis d'Hervey de Saint-Denis, Paris, 1867; 17–18 The Astral Light, cover illustrations from *The Art and Practice of Astral Projection*, by Ophiel, New York, 1961; see pp. 92–93.)

19, 20 Dreams mediate between levels of reality, and the process of transition may be indicated, positively or negatively, by images of ascent into light or descent into darkness. A total reconstruction of the Self is made possible through the acceptance of psychic terror and symbolic death in the dream state, and this knowledge has been preserved in shamanistic traditions from Greenland to Malaysia. The Chuckchi explicitly recognize the two-way traffic through the levels of middle earth, the infernal regions and the heavens. Maps (left) show the way and minimize the risk of becoming lost. Paths to the worlds of dawn, of evening and of darkness pass through the pole star, the axis of the world, while sun, moon, planets and stars shine simultaneously.

Western culture, in contrast, has provided few maps to the dark regions of the psyche. The French illustrator Grandville, who produced the dream picture above shortly before his death, expressed ideas of despair and disorientation which contrast strongly with the Chuckchi sense of direction and choice. (19 Chuckchi drawing, Siberia, USSR; 20 Crime and Punishment, wood engraving after J. J. Grandville, published posthumously in *Le Magasin pittoresque*, France, 1847.)

The flyer.

21, 22 Images of flight and ascension are metaphors for transcendence and spiritual freedom. In this sense, the dream of flying, which implies a desire to abolish time and space and to unify matter and spirit, is a basic part of human nature, symbolizing the need, and perhaps the possibility, of becoming free from all conditioned limitations.

The shaman (above) *deliberately* cultivates this state. His costume and stance imitate the qualities of birds: in his transformation he *is* a bird; his soul has wings. The legend of Usha's dream flight (right) describes a *spontaneous* experience from which she returns with information that can be verified on the level of everyday reality. (21 The Flyer, watercolour by John White from Virginia series, England, *c.* 1585–90; 22 Usha, miniature from the *Bhagavata Purana*, Kangra, India, early 19th c.)

23, 24 The sleeping dreamer is overwhelmed by experiences of the forces of the unknown (above). The awakened dreamer confronts these forces and they become allies. Certain traditions (right) teach that to be conscious in one's dreams, to be aware and in control during sleep, is part of the process leading to enlightenment. (23 The Sleep of Reason Begets Monsters, etching from *Los Caprichos* by Francisco de Goya, Spain, *c.* 1810–15; 24 Arhat Dreaming, Buddhist scroll painting, China, 18th c.)

25, 26 Some esoteric traditions of Islam speak of seven levels or stages of the human personality and its development. These stages, sometimes called 'men' (left), are degrees in the transformation of consciousness, considered 'asleep' until it is deliberately 'awakened'.

Ordinary unfulfilled consciousness is restructured through a process described as 'awakening the *lataif*', the five organs of spiritual perception. In this dish from Kashan (below), the unconscious dreamer is shown about to awaken, as the presence of the five princes indicates. His dream suggests the possibility of regeneration through recognizing the dynamic, intuitive, female side of his personality, and acknowledging the reality of the spiritual world behind the world of appearances. (25 The Seven Sleepers, manuscript illumination from *History of the Prophets*, by Nishapuri, Iran, *c.* 1550; 26 Kashan lustre dish, Iran, *c.* 1210.)

27, 28 Hypnos and Thanatos, Sleep and Death, carry off a dead hero's body (left). Sleep and death are twins (see pl. 3), two representations of the same condition of the self, just as waking, living and conscious dreaming are different modes of the opposite condition. This mystery was expressed concisely by the ancient Egyptians, whose word for dream derived from the verb 'to awaken'. Here, the *ba* (right), one of the three spiritual aspects of the human being, hovers over the

dead initiate in the form of a jabiru-bird. It was
believed that the *ba* left the body in dreams and in
death, and remained lucid, dynamic and adventurous
in the spiritual realms which were its permanent home.
(27 Hypnos and Thanatos, Attic red-figure kylix-
krater by Euphronius, Greece, 520–510 BC; 28 *Ba* and
the Mummy, from the papyrus of Ani, Theban Book
of the Dead, Egypt, *c*. 1250 BC.)

29 In the New Testament, Christ's conception is revealed to Joseph in a dream, but is announced directly to Mary while she is awake. Although these biblical visions have been formalized to accommodate a specific religious tradition, the idea that God was more accessible to human nature in the dream than in the waking vision was widespread in the ancient world. Only those who are, by nature or training, more spiritually advanced, closer to God, and so less tied to the materiality of the world, were believed able to receive a vision while awake. In the dream, when the perceptions of the ordinary senses are naturally subdued, people are more amenable to God, and more easily able to accept a vision without damaging their sense of reality. (29 Panel of the Werden ivory casket, north-west Germany, early 9th c. AD.)

30, 31 The symbolism of the alchemists records their efforts to achieve their own spiritual regeneration, through a process of transmutation. This quest is often represented as a dream in which the meaning of cryptic and allegorical figures and events is either guessed successfully by the dreamer or explained by a character within the dream. The author of 'Three Dreams of the Transmutation of Metals' (below) shows himself dreaming with his eyes open, suggesting his complete lucidity. A similar image, of the awakening of the self from its dream, occurs in popular Christian tradition. Wise men from the East, the first Gentiles to worship the infant Christ, were 'warned of God in a dream'. The number of the wise men is not mentioned by St Matthew, but they are traditionally known as the Three Kings, and represent the three aspects of human nature: soul, mind and body. Here (right), each is shown in a different stage of awakening, as God's angel points to their star. Two episodes of their story are combined and transformed in this image of the awakening of the self. (30 The Dreamer, woodcut from *Della transmutatione metallica sogni tre*, by Giovanni Battista Nazari, Brescia, 1599; 31 Capital by Gislebertus from the church of Saint-Lazare, Autun, France, early 12th c.)

32, 33 Dreams which mark a stage on the path of illumination are recorded in all cultures. St Ursula's vocation, martyrdom and glory were announced to her in a dream; Mohammed's prophetic mission was revealed to him in a series of night visions in which the Archangel Gabriel appeared to him as a guide (see pl. 49). Angels, symbols of invisible forces, of the powers ascending and descending between the source of life and the world of phenomena, were said by the Muslim mystic al'Ghazali to represent 'the higher faculties in human nature'. Communication between these faculties and the mundane self results in the great dreams of prophets, saints and mystics, in which potentials for transcendence and freedom are formalized in mythic terms relevant to an entire society. (32 The Dream of St Ursula, painting by Vittore Carpaccio, Italy, early 16th c.; 33 Gabriel Appearing to Mohammed, from *The Night Journey*, Herat, Iran, 15th c.)

34, 35 When King Nebuchadnezzar called on his magicians, sorcerers and astrologers to interpret a dream (above) he could not recall, Daniel recovered the lost information in a divinely inspired night vision and was able to interpret it correctly.

The Iroquois considered dreams the language of the soul, the way in which it expresses its needs. They understood that a dream may conceal as well as reveal, and specific procedures were followed in order 'to see the natural and hidden desires the soul has . . . although he who may have had the dreams has completely forgotten them'. Regular formal ceremonies were held to gratify dream wishes; for those who had forgotten their dreams, dream-guessing ceremonies in which cornhusk masks (right) were worn were held twice a year in each village. (34 The Dream of Nebuchadnezzar, from *Speculum humanae salvationis*, 15th c.; 35 Iroquois mask, New York, USA, c. 1915.)

36, 37 The dream mediates between invisible potentials and experienced reality. On the highest levels it is the process by which the invisible is made manifest, becoming capable of action in the material world. The Dream of Maya, the Blessed One's future mother, is the true conception and incarnation of the Buddha, as the Dream of the Virgin is the true conception and incarnation of the Christ. Outside time, matter is united with spirit, and the eternal enters into and transforms history. (36 The Dream of the Blessed Virgin, painting by Simone dei Crocifissi, Italy, 14th c.; 37 The Dream of Maya, painting, China, 10th c.)

38, 39 A sense of the dream state as the link between the worlds of matter and spirit is characteristic of entire societies where individual consciousness is encouraged to acknowledge unthinkable potentials. Such perceptions of the ultimate wholeness of reality may be formalized in precise notations. The diagram on a shaman's drum maps his or her cosmic journey through the centre of the three worlds, while the drum itself projects the primal sound which orders the cosmos and induces the state of ecstasy in which the dream journey may be consciously repeated.

The Australians consider the Eternal Dreamtime as an era in which humans and nature came to be as they are now: yet the Dreamtime is contemporary and inextricably connected with the events of mundane history. *Churinga* are secret, numinous, occult maps of Dreamtime events seen from the point of view of the spiritual essence of the individual, that part of the self which exists outside time. (38 Lapp shaman's drum; 39 *Churinga*, Ngalia tribe, central Australia; see pp. 94–95.)

40, 41 The entire world may be understood as the dream of an awakened dreamer. In dreams of this order there is, literally, no distinction between levels of reality. Spiritual and material aspects of the world come into existence together, and are perceived and created simultaneously. Emanation is equated with realization. The creative principle of the world grows out of the navel of the dreaming god (above) in the mythical instant of the creation of the universe. This concept is present in the shamanic tradition, perhaps as old as human history, in which the individual adept assumes the role of conscious creator. Here (left) the bird-staff symbolizes the autonomy and lucidity of the Palaeolithic shaman, who creates the desired animal by dreaming, and attacks it with psychic weapons. (40 Cave painting, Lascaux, France, Upper Palaeolithic; 41 Krishna acting out the role of Vishnu in his sleep, gouache, India, 18th c.)

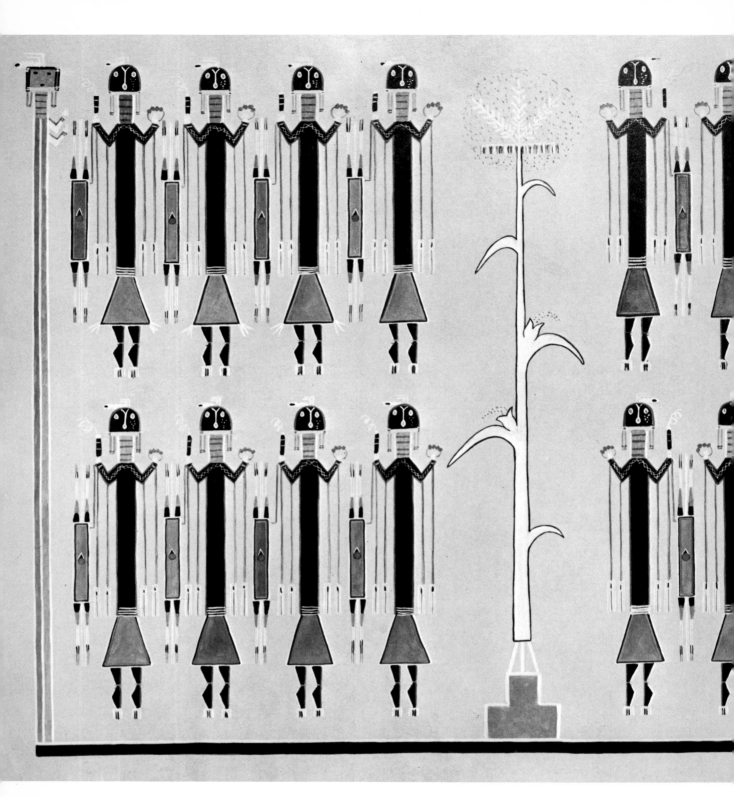

42, 43, 44 Myths are dreams, great dreams whose reality is of a numinous order. They are institutionalized in ceremonies and rituals which are themselves the means of abolishing the limitations of time and space, recreating the original wholeness of reality. The myths on which the Navajo Nightway chant is based are said to record the dreams and visions of Bĭtáhĭni, the Dreamer. All aspects of the nine-day ritual – its dances, music, colours, incense, recipes, masks, sandpaintings and cures – were revealed to him in this way. Participants in the ceremony recreate the essential attributes of the main actors in this dreamed world. The

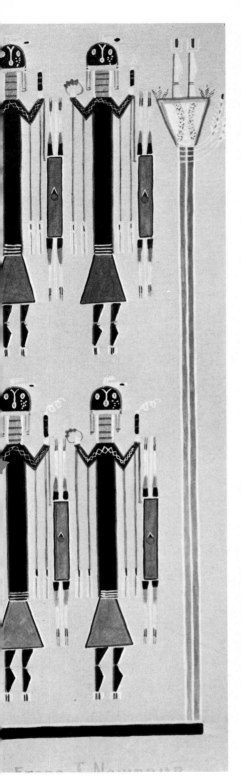

Yébĭtsai or Grandfather of the Gods, a prominent figure in the ceremonies, manipulates a talisman (right), itself a numinous object that the
chanter receives from his teacher, keeps all his life and transmits to a
pupil. The fourfold form of the talisman and related sandpainting (left)
indicates a profound understanding of the apparent gulf between the
material and spiritual worlds, symbolizing the mundane manifestation
of an ideal wholeness. (42 Fourth sandpainting from the Navajo Nightway chant, by Hosteen Klah, New Mexico, USA, before 1932, copy by
Franc J. Newcomb; 43, 44 Talisman of Yébĭtsai from Nightway chant.)

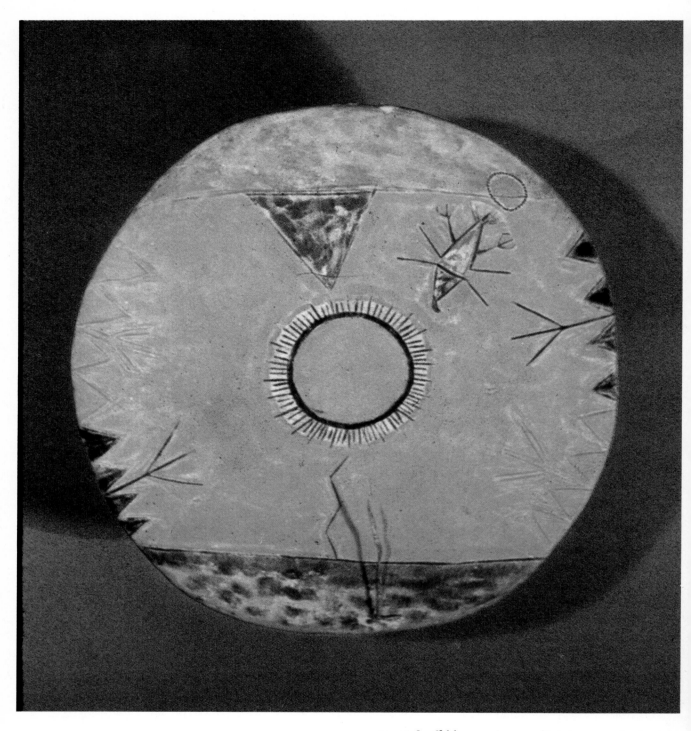

45, 46 Ineffable experiences of brightness and splendour have been related by dreamers in many traditions. To become illuminated, to achieve enlightenment, means to become aware of the source of light. This shield motif (above) is a token of a dream, a formalized reference to the owner's celestial patron. The shield is a vehicle for recreating the awareness of the self as a spiritual and therefore invulnerable being, just as the Tantric painting (right) is at one and the same time a symbol of an experience of absolute wholeness and a meditation object used for re-entering the ultimate state. (45 Apache buckskin shield, New Mexico, USA, 1860–80; 46 The Primal Light, gouache and gold on paper, India, 18th c.)

47, 48 The shaman, who exists lucidly and autonomously in dreams as in waking life, is shown (below) at the centre of two concentric circles representing everyday reality enclosed within the world of spirit. Yet, beyond this, attributes symbolizing his or her conscious control and dynamism project further into the unknown, suggesting the possibility of transcending all definitions and limitations. Tibetan temples contain pictorial representations of the six realms of the illusory world, in the form of a wheel (right). The segments represent the six main types of worldly, unenlightened existence, which are created by the delusions that follow from falsely identifying ego-consciousness with true consciousness. The seeker must understand the illusions of the waking state before proceeding to explore the more subtle illusions of the dream state. It is more difficult to understand the illusory nature of dreams because it is possible superficially to equate their immateriality with unreality, instead of recognizing immateriality itself as a further illusion to be penetrated. To grasp this paradox fully marks a decisive step on the path to liberation from the endless cycles of death and rebirth. (47 Eskimo wooden mask, Nunivak Island, Greenland; 48 The Wheel of Life, woodcut, Tibet, early 20th c.)

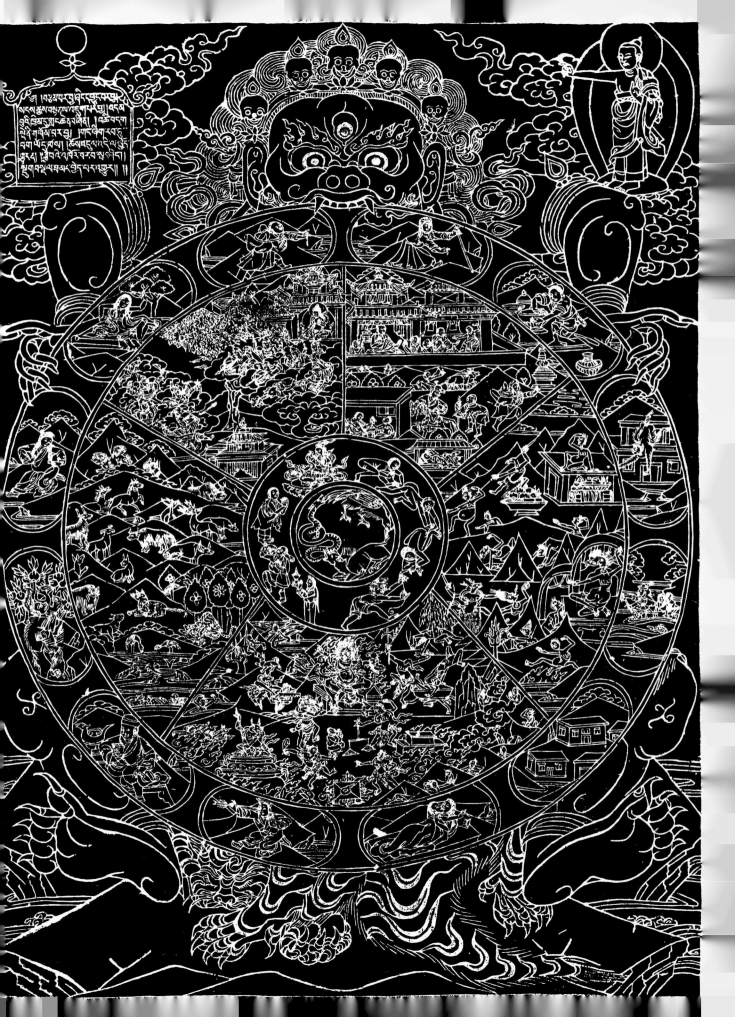

49 The *Lailatal-Miraj*, or Night Journey, the Prophet Mohammed's great dream of initiation into the mysteries of the cosmos, began as he was sleeping between the hills of Safa and Meeva, when the Angel Gabriel approached, leading Elboraq, the half-human silver mare, who carried him in an instant to Jerusalem, the centre of the world. Descending into the depths of hell, and ascending through the seven celestial spheres whose esoteric meanings correspond to the seven levels of existence, he passed through oceans of white light, finally to approach God. Lucid and ecstatic, the dreamer has reached the highest level of human development. (49 The Ascent of the Prophet Mohammed, from the *Khamseh* of Nizami, India, 16th c.)

Documentary illustrations and commentaries

1 The personification of dreams, with Jacob's Ladder. (Engraving by J. Wachsmuth after Eichler, Germany, 18th c., from Cesare Ripa, *Iconologia*, 1758–60.)

Dream systems

Each human society puts a different value on the dream and its function. When the material world is seen as ultimately real, the dream is reduced either to fantasy or to physiology; when the non-material or spiritual is considered to be of primary importance, the dream is highly valued for its own sake. Conceptual systems that attempt to integrate inner and outer perceptions stress the continuity of conscious awareness uniting dream life and waking life.

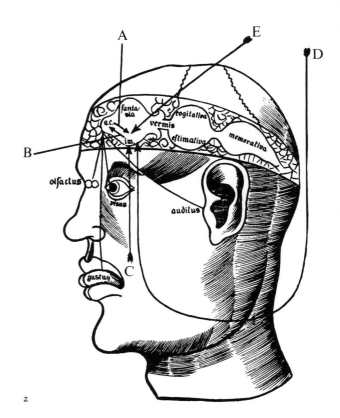

2

2 This schematic representation is based on Aristotle's opinion that dreams have a physiological basis (see p. 6). As Robert Burton stated in *The Anatomy of Melancholy* (1621): 'Imagination . . . is an inner sense which doth more fully examine the species perceived by the common sense, of things present or absent, and keeps them longer, recalling them to mind again, or making new of his own. In time of sleep, this faculty is free, and many time conceive of strange, stupend, absurd shapes. . . . His organ is the middle cell of the brain. . . . Dreams . . . vary according to humours, diet, actions, objects, etc.' (Diagram of the dream process: A, direction of the process of cognition; B, direction of the dream process; C, influences from the body; D, influences from the stars, which act only through the body; E, influences from the rational soul. After G. Reisch, *Margarita mundi*, Strasbourg, 1504, and Paul Diepgen, *Traum und Traumdeutung . . . im Mittelalter*, Berlin, 1912.)

3 Theories which define the dream as a conditioned physiological response underlie recent experimental work on the biology of dreaming. Michel Jouvet has identified the *pons* as the brain centre which inhibits stimulation of muscles during dreaming and so stops the body from moving and acting out its dream. Jouvet suggests that although people differ in what they dream most frequently, the instincts underlying common dreams are the same for everyone, and the function of dreaming is to 'practise' these instincts. (From *The Sunday Times*, London, 23 September 1973.)

4 Indian traditions recognize the paradox of the 'reality' of dreams, which parallels the 'reality' of waking life, by ultimately relegating both to the status of illusion. To achieve enlightenment, it is necessary to penetrate each of the three preliminary states of consciousness (waking, dreaming and dreamless sleep) represented by the letters of the essential mantra AUM. One must pass through these states in complete lucidity without any discontinuity of consciousness. (Om or Aum, Tibet, from Anagarika Govinda, *Foundations of Tibetan Mysticism*, London 1960; see also pl. 4.)

5 Night (Nyx) holds the infant twins Sleep (Hypnos) and Death (Thanatos) in her arms. Morpheus, god of dreams, descends holding a smoking horn and a stave, symbols of false and true dreams. In Greek mythology, Sleep, Dream and Death, genealogically only one generation removed from Chaos, preceded the Olympic Gods in order of existence. (Night and Dream, woodcut from Vincenzo Cartari, *Le imagini de i dei . . .*, Lyons, 1581; see pl. 3.)

6 The ancient Egyptians considered sleep a rehearsal for death, and in dreams aspects of the self were believed to wander in and out of paradisal or hellish realms guarded by terrible watchmen – the same realms where the soul, at death, would ultimately have to find its way. Paths through them were mapped according to information based on myth and dreams, and placed at the feet of the dead with instructions reading, 'You must not go this way,' or 'This is the way of the living person.' (Detail of papyrus of Ani, Egypt, *c.* 1250 BC; see also pl. 28.)

5

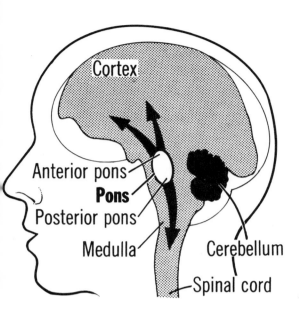

3

4

Dream incubation

The practice of dream incubation, in which dreams are obtained by sleeping at a sacred site dedicated to the cult of a particular spirit or divinity, is widespread. The natural site, a peak or 'holy mountain', was formerly used for dream incubation in Tibet and Nepal within the context of Bon, the pre-Buddhist religion of the Himalayas, and also by numerous American Indian cultures. In these cases, the incubated dream was probably sought as a means of access to spiritual knowledge, to a way of power. Later cultures marked such sacred sites by a temple or a church, as an outward sign of the inner experience. Dream incubation reached a height of popularity in Egypt and in Greece in the 2nd and 3rd centuries AD, when it had become merely a request for physical healing through the dream. Mostly in this sense, dream incubation continued, in the Eastern Christian Church in Cyprus and at Constantinople, and, according to St Gregory of Tours, in the Roman Catholic Church at Saint-Martin de Tours and Saint-Julien de Brioude in France. It was practised in the 17th and 18th centuries in Italy and Austria, and is still practised today in Lebanon, Greece, India and North Africa.

The process of ritual purification required in the Asklepian temples of 2nd-century Greece has already been discussed (p.18); the following example quoted by Ania Teillard describes 20th-century rites of preparation and purification for an incubated dream in an Indian temple at Mahabalipuram dedicated to the goddess Parvathi, who gives children to barren women:

'Sita Lakshmi . . . was obliged to dedicate herself entirely to the service of the goddess. . . . She was allowed one meal a day, and a little milk and fruit in the evening. Morning and night, she made the round of the temple one hundred and eight times, imploring the goddess to hear her and calling her by her innumerable names. As is customary, to avoid any mistake, at each round she put a little pebble in a small sack hanging from a tree. This time of preparation lasted six months.

'When the six months came to an end she was to make the round of the temple for the last time; she must not walk, but roll round it on the rocky ground. Her parents were obliged to help her for she could not do it alone.

'At last the decisive moment arrived. Sita Lakshmi . . . was led by the priests into the temple. There, behind the altar, was a stone bench where the suppliant must await in a holy sleep the judgment of the goddess. . . Lying on the hard bench, she implored the goddess with fervent prayers until the moment of sleep.

'Then she had a dream: an aged priest came to her bearing a bronze tray with four coconuts, three large and one small. He offered the tray to her, casting the small coconut on the ground, where it was broken into pieces.

'The priests interpreted her dream for her. She was to give birth to four children, but one of them would die young.' (Ania Teillard, *Spiritual Dimensions*, London, 1961.)

The incubated dream and its interpretation proved correct.

7 Temple dedicated to Yakushi, the Bodhisattva master of healing, Nara, Japan, founded AD 680.

8 Temple dedicated to Parvathi, Mahabalipuram, India, *c*. AD 700.

9 Temple of Hygeia, ancient incubation site, Palermo, Sicily.

10 Marabouts' shrines, in use as incubation sites, Morocco.

11 Church in use as an incubation site, Tinos, Greece.

7

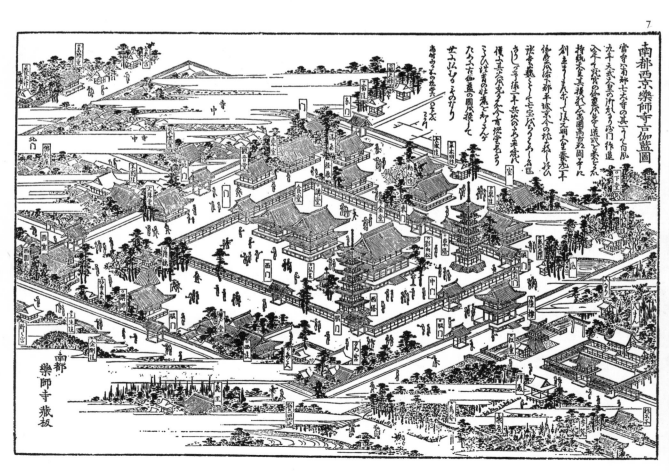

8

9

10

11

Induced dreams

Significant or desired dreams can be deliberately induced by a variety of methods: isolation, fasting, magic, ritual, drugs, incubation, or more usually, by various combinations of these methods. The use of fasting and isolation to induce certain dreams or dream states was common in the vision quest practices of the American Plains Indians: 'At the age of fourteen or fifteen, the Indian boy . . . retires to some solitary place and remains for days without food. . . . His sleep is haunted by visions, and the form which first or most often appears is that of his guardian *manitou*. . . . An eagle or a bear is the vision of a destined warrior; a wolf, of a successful hunter; while a serpent foreshadows the future medicine-man.' (Francis Parkman, *Indian Superstitions*, Cedar Falls, 1866.) The use of these methods in a Tibetan context has been discussed on p. 14.

The biblical story of St Joachim, the father of the Virgin Mary, is in some respects a comparable example of the use of fasting and isolation to induce a desired dream: after twenty years of childless marriage, Joachim went by chance to make offering at the Temple in Jerusalem, but the High Priest refused to accept his offering and drove him away; for, according to the Scriptures, 'cursed is every man who does not beget a man child in Israel. And Joachim . . . retired to the wilderness and fixed his tent there, and fasted 40 days and 40 nights. And at the end of the time an angel appeared and told him he should bring forth a daughter, and she should be named Mary.' (*Apocryphal Gospel of the Birth of Mary*.)

12 Hashish is used by *saddhus* in India to induce intense dream perceptions; wine was formerly used by heretical Muslim groups in Nuristan, in eastern Afghanistan. In the Americas, the use of peyote to induce ecstatic dreams and visions is found in the Southwest United States and in Mexico. The petroglyphs in Lewis Canyon, Texas, are reported to have been created by Indians who ceremonially ate mescal buttons (peyote), slept for twenty-four hours and, on waking, recorded their sleeping visions on the rock face. (Petroglyphs, Lewis Canyon, copy by F. Kirkland, from W. W. Newcomb Jr, *The Rock Art of Texas Indians*, University of Texas Press, Austin, 1938. Courtesy of the Texas Memorial Museum, Austin, Tex.)

13 The use of magical objects to induce dreams is shown in this European woodcut: 'He or she who looked at Zizaa, a precious stone, was said to have marvellous dreams.' (Woodcut from *Ortus sanitatis*, 1491.)

14 The Dream of St Joachim. (Painting by Giotto; Scrovegni Chapel, Padua, Italy, early 14th c.)

15 Amphiaraos, who foresaw the outcome of the war against Thebes in a prophetic dream, was later made immortal, and the temple dedicated to him at Oropos became famous as a site for inducing and interpreting dreams. In this votive relief erected by Archinos, a grateful recipient of the god's power, the dreamer is shown asleep, tended by a priest, while in his dream Amphiaraos heals his wounds. (Votive relief from Oropos, Greece, National Museum, Athens.)

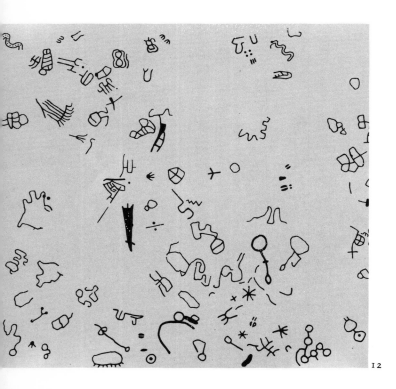

12

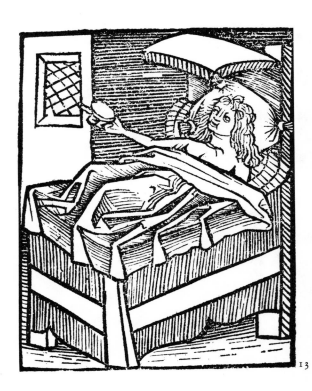

13

14

15

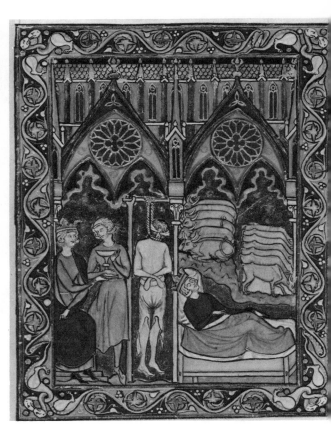

16

19

20

Dream interpretation

When dreams are perceived as a reality, the dreamer does not usually require an interpretation of the experience. Nor is an interpretation required when dreams are perceived as unreal, for unreality is usually understood to be meaningless. It is when the perception of the dream falls into the gap between reality and unreality, when the dream is seen as real but of a different – spiritual, psychic, symbolic or magical – reality, that the dreamer feels in need of an interpretation.

To fulfil this need, many societies have produced a class of professional dream interpreters who, in conjunction with religious, magical or medical theories, attempt to explain the dreams of their patients/clients. The Brahmin oneirocritics in India, the *om myoshi* in Japan, the Hasidic rabbis in Europe, the Egyptian *pa-hery-tep*, the priests of Greek incubation cults, and the contemporary psychotherapists, have all functioned as dream interpreters within their respective cultural systems.

An extension of this social role has been the publication of dream books by interpreters who have attempted somewhat ethnocentrically to establish an objective correlation between dream images and specific objects, actions or emotions in the waking state. The ultimate failure of any given system of dream interpretation lies in a twofold paradox. The dreamer who needs to have dreams interpreted suffers from a lack of psychic unity, but when he or she seeks an outside interpretation this disunity is reinforced rather than overcome: the best that an oneirocritic can achieve is to teach the dreamer to understand his or her own dreams, to find an interpretation that is subjectively satisfying. Again, any system of dream interpretation functions adequately in its own terms, and therefore, once the dreamer accepts the system to the extent of taking part in its process, any interpretation will be 'true'; and if any interpretation is true, then every interpretation is true.

16 The Buddha's future mother dreamed that a brilliant white elephant with six tusks entered her womb. The Brahmins interpreted her dream to mean 'superabundance of joy. . . . A son will be born to Maya. . . . Issue of a royal line, the magnanimous one will be a universal monarch [and,] detached by compassion for the three worlds, he will become a wandering monk.' (Limestone relief from the Stupa, Amaravata, India, *c*. AD 150–200; see pl. 37.)

17 Pharaoh's dream of the seven fat and seven lean kine was successfully interpreted by Joseph, who had previously given true explanations of the dreams of Pharaoh's baker and wine steward, whose similar dreams were related to distinctly different events in their lives (Gen. 40–41). (Pharaoh's Dream, from Psalter of St Louis, France, 13th c., Bibliothèque Nationale, Paris.)

18 Among the Aztecs, dream interpretation and divination by dreams were the prerogative of the priestly class *teopexqui*, the Masters of the Secret Things; and, among the Maya, of the *cocome*, the Listeners. (Itzcoliuhqui makes offering before the House of Darkness, from the Codex Cospiano, Bologna.)

19 The Chester Beatty papyrus contains records of 200 dreams and their interpretations according to the priests of the god Horus. A companion collection compiled by the priests of Set has been lost, and there is now no way of knowing to what extent these schools of interpretation differed. (From Chester Beatty papyrus, Egypt, *c*. 1250 BC, British Museum, London.)

20 Despite their triviality, dream books of this kind (first made *c*. AD 200) reflect a universal popular awareness of the significance of dreams. (*The Dreamer's True Friend*, London, 1874.)

21

22

23

Dream artifacts (1)

The Saora of Orissa, India, create a sacred art on the walls of their houses using information obtained in dreams. The pictographs, called *ittal* (writing), are made to honour the dead or to cure disease. They establish and commemorate situations in which the inhabitants of the spiritual worlds communicate with the people of this world. The theme of the *ittal* is usually a 'house', represented by a rectangle or square, a two-dimensional home for a spiritual being. This miniature temple constitutes a sacred space on a wall which previously functioned merely as the boundary of a mundane area where everyday activities occur. The *ittal* transforms the wall, reducing the opacity of the border between the spiritual worlds and the material world.

Anyone may paint an *ittal*. The householder may do so, following instructions given in a dream; but, if the dream does not specify the form the picture is to take, a recognized specialist, the *ittalmaran,* will be asked to prepare to receive this in a deliberately sought dream. Until such a dream occurs, the artist may not eat, and will sleep by the wall where the picture is to be painted. As soon as the dream has taken place, the *ittal* is quickly drawn, and when the first draft is complete a shaman is asked to invoke the being in whose honour it was made. The shaman, in trance, speaks with the spirit's voice, criticizing or praising the accuracy of the artist's work, and suggesting modifications which are incorporated in the final version of the *ittal*. (Illustrations from H.V. Elwin, *Tribal Art of Middle India*, Oxford, 1951.)

21 This *ittal* was painted to cure a woman of a nervous breakdown attributed to the god Jaliyasum. Her husband dreamed the design, representing the marriage feast of Jaliyasum, who is appeased by representations of his wealth and prestige. (From house at Kattumeru, Ganjam District, Orissa, India.)

22 This pictograph shows the house of a deity, with additional material relating to the night journeys of the male shaman. The *Ittal* was painted to honour the shaman's spirit-wife, who is shown in sexual intercourse with the shaman, represented by a couple who share one body. Their union is creative, indicated by the two spirit-children riding an elephant. (From the house of Gamru, Boraisingi, Ganjam District, Orissa, India.)

23 A female shaman's spirit-husband with his own spirit-helper and their assistants. The two small figures at bottom right may represent the spirit-children of the shaman, who visit her in dreams. (From the house of Tissano, Tumalu, Ganjam District, Orissa, India.)

24

25

26

24 This pictograph was painted to appease a dead husband, who threatened in a dream to make the crops fail unless his wife asked for an *ittal* picturing his situation in the spirit world. It shows the house of a deity, with the train and motor-car by which the man's ghost travels. (From house in Orissa, India.)

25 This pictograph is from the house of a male shaman who had married two spirit-wives who did not agree and refused to assist him. He dreamed a large house where both of them lived contentedly together, as shown here. (From the house of Dalimo, shaman of Karubai, Koraput District, Orissa, India.)

26 This pictograph illustrates the harmonious relations between shamans and their spirit-mates. (From house at Potta, Koraput District, Orissa, India.)

Dream artifacts (2)

The Chippewa (Ojibway) of the northern United States and Canada consciously cultivated the ability to dream: 'In the old days our people had no education. They could not learn from books or teachers. All their wisdom and knowledge came to them in dreams. They tested their dreams and in that way learned their own strength.' Wisdom and knowledge – the ability to heal, courage, creativity, and all other attributes considered valuable in human nature – were received as a form of grace in dreams or visions. Children were encouraged from early childhood to try to dream and to remember their dreams. It is not clear whether Chippewa women deliberately sought visionary experience, although it is known that they frequently received 'wisdom and knowledge' in dreams; but at puberty each Chippewa boy fasted for four days in solitude and reverence, preparing for an experience that would determine his future. The revelation would come in a dream or vision, expressed in the form of a song he would sing only in battle, when he was facing death. After enforced reservation life made going to war a thing of the past, the songs remained unsung. Such a song was a reservoir of unused strength, and in order to avert the threat of being slowly destroyed by his own 'power', the Chippewa who had a vision he was unable to use would erect a special pole. On the pole he would fasten a cloth on which was painted the cryptic symbol of his dream – sun, moon, star or bird. Everyone recognized that in a house before which stood such a pole lived someone who was never able to sing his song, but who had the power to heal and to face death.

27 This woman's talisman is a mnemonic for a dream like the one referred to in this Chippewa dream song, quoted by Francis Densmore in *Chippewa Music* (Washington, 1910): 'In the sky/ I am walking,/ A bird/ I accompany.' The dream talisman and the dream song are both devices for recreating the original moment of heightened perception, the condition of direct communication with the sacred. (Chippewa talisman from White Earth, Minnesota, USA.)

28 These beadwork motifs are symbolic references to 'wisdom and knowledge' dreams of Chippewa women. (Chippewa beadwork from Minnesota, USA.)

29 Dream flag with a bear, used by a man to cure his wife by wrapping her in it. (Chippewa, Mille Lacs, Minnesota, USA.)

30 Man's dream flag. (Chippewa, White Earth, Minnesota, USA.)

31 Kĭ′tciödja′nimwewgĭ′jig's dream flag. (Chippewa, Lac du Flambeau, Wisconsin, USA.)

32 Dream flag and pole in front of a house on a Chippewa Reservation. (Lac du Flambeau, Wisconsin, USA.)

27

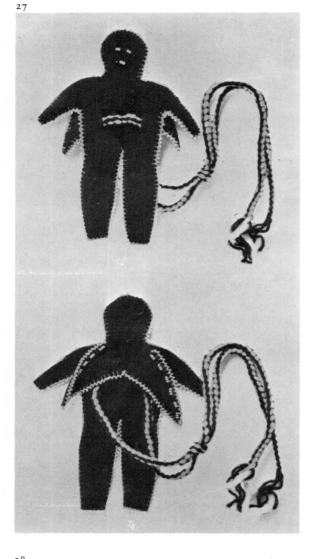

28

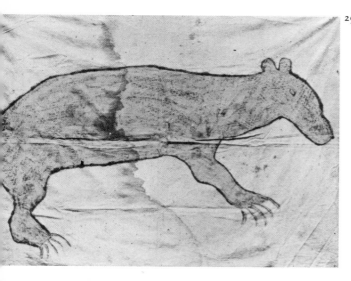

29

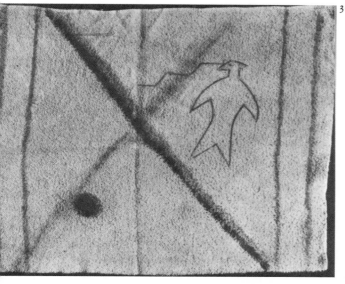

30

32

31

85

33

To return from the dream state with new knowledge or insight, or with an archetypal or significant image, is the object of all creative dreaming. The creative dreamer recognizes the value of both the dream state and the waking state; they are two distinct modes of perception, and the dream artifact serves as a bridge between them.

33, 34 The archetypal image of Ouroboros, the snake swallowing its tail, was used by the alchemists to represent creative energy in its most cosmic aspects. According to his own description, the German chemist F. A. Kekulé discovered the formula for benzene as a result of seeing this image in a dream (see p. 16). (33 Ouroboros, after an alchemical manuscript, Venice, 14th c. AD; 34 Diagram of benzene molecule, C_6H_6.)

34

35

36

37

35 The contemporary western society in which the dreamer of this version of the Four World Directions lived suggested no significant cultural or spiritual use for his dream image, and it remained a personal 'totem' in the form of a bookplate. (Illustration from J. S. Lincoln, *The Dream in Primitive Cultures*, London, 1935.)

36 Like the dreamer of the Ghost Dance dress (pl. 12), Mrs Wright received this design in an ecstatic dream. In a setting 'filled with bright light', her analyst's wife appeared, her eyes like stars. 'She said to me, "I will show you your room." Then she showed me into one of the rooms where there was a bed and on it a night costume finely embroidered with lace. I said, "That costume is too fine for me. A plain one would do." But she said, "That is your costume."' Mrs Wright woke up repeating the words of a Rescue Mission hymn: 'Palms of victory, crowns of glory, / Palms of victory I shall see.' (From John Layard, *The Lady of the Hare*, London, 1954.)

37 Among the Plains Indians, the guardian spirit encountered in the vision quest instructed the dreamer how to dress in battle and what medicines to use as curing aids, or taught him a sacred song. On waking, the dreamer often made a talisman containing a cryptic reference to his experience, which served as a means of recalling or recreating it. Besides celestial patrons in the form of animals or birds, the dreamer might encounter an abstract but no less real guardian spirit such as the Four World Directions suggested by this drum motif. (Mandan buffalo hide drum, North Dakota, USA.)

38 Eskimo shamans describe the creatures and entities who inhabit the dream world, and masks representing these are created for use in public ceremonies. This mask, made of driftwood and painted in soft colours, illustrates the *inua*, or inner spirit, of the seal. All beings are said to have an *inua*, but this can be perceived only in states of heightened awareness. (Eskimo wooden mask, Good News Bay, Alaska, USA.)

38

Dream art (1)

In 1924, André Breton, poet, theoretician and co-founder of Surrealism, called for the recognition of the forces of the unconscious. Great emphasis is placed on the dream in the *Manifeste du surréalisme*: it is understood as the realization of the natural, the illogical, the hidden, the secret human truths. The dream that Breton refers to is the Freudian dream, the 'royal road to the unconscious'. He was not as interested in the dream state itself as in the dream as a means of access to the irrational: 'Perhaps the imagination is on the verge of recovering its rights. If the depths of our minds conceal strange forces capable of augmenting or conquering those on the surface, it is in our greatest interest to capture them; first to capture them and later to submit them, should the occasion arise, to the control of reason.' Although popular opinion has accepted Surrealist painting as 'dream art' without making any distinction between 'dream' and 'dream-like', it is important to attempt to distinguish the ways in which the work of the various artists gathered together under the name of Surrealism is related to the dream state.

The first Surrealist poets (for at its origins the movement was primarily a literary one) had experimented with automatic writing, produced in a trance, and consequently without regard for logical, literary or social conventions. Visual extensions of these experiments were made by the painter André Masson, who produced a series of automatic drawings (see pl. 15).

Jean Arp, poet, painter and sculptor, came to Surrealism from Dada after making the first of his 'dreamed plastic works' (see pl. 14). 'I believe', he wrote, 'that nature is not in opposition to art. Art is of natural origin and is sublimated and spiritualized through the sublimation of man.' Through the dream, Arp was able to reach the sublimated pure form.

39 Giorgio de Chirico, who was hailed as a master and precursor by the Surrealists, saw the dream as an ideal, if unconscious, state: 'If a work of art is to be truly immortal, it must pass quite beyond the limits of the human world, without any sign of common sense and logic. In this way the work will draw nearer to the dream. . . .

'We should keep constant control of our thoughts and of all the images that present themselves to our minds . . . which . . . have a close relationship with those we see in dreams. It is curious that in dreams, no image, however strange it may be, ever strikes us because of its metaphysical strength; and therefore we flee from seeking a source of inspiration in the dream – the methods of people like Thomas de Quincey do not tempt us. Yet the dream is an extremely strange phenomenon and an inexplicable mystery'. (Massimo Carrà (ed.), *Metaphysical Art*, London and New York, 1971.) (The Pink Tower, painting by Giorgio de Chirico, Italy, 1913, Peggy Guggenheim Foundation, Venice.)

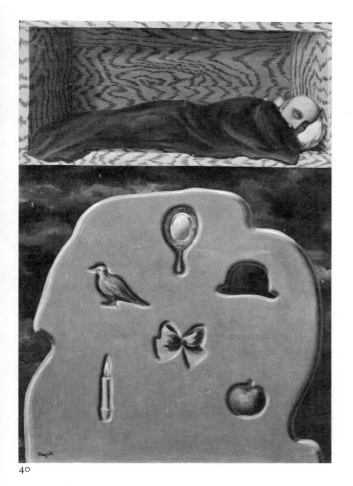

40

40 René Magritte: 'The word "dream" is often misused concerning my painting. We certainly wish the realm of dreams to be respectable – but our works are not oneiric. *On the contrary.* If "dreams" are concerned in this context, they are very different from those we have while sleeping. It is a question rather of *self-willed* "dreams", in which nothing is as vague as those feelings one has when escaping in dreams.' (Suzi Gablik, *Magritte*, London and New York, 1970.) Magritte's paintings discover moments of paradoxical clarity; they are artificial dreams. (The Reckless Sleeper, painting by René Magritte, Belgium, 1927, Tate Gallery, London.)

41 'It was in 1929', writes Salvador Dali, 'that Salvador Dali fixed his attention on the internal mechanisms of paranoiac phenomena . . . this method subsequently became the delirious-critical synthesis which bears the name "paranoiac-critical activity". Paranoia: delirium of interpretive association permitting a systemic structure. Paranoiac-critical activity: spontaneous method of irrational understanding based upon the interpretive critical association of delirious phenomena.' (Patrick Waldberg, *Surrealism*, London and New York, 1965.) The art of Dali consists of figurative depiction of a highly stylized 'dream-world' that pays open homage to the Freudian revolution of the time. (The Great Dreamer, or, The Great Paranoiac, painting by Salvador Dali, Spain, 1936, Tate Gallery, London.)

41

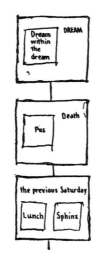

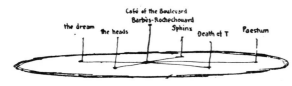

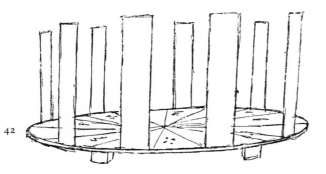

Dream art (2)

There are many different ways in which art can be related to the dream state. Jasper Johns' first flag painting, reputedly the result of a dream, is, despite its innovatory importance in the art of the mid 1950s, a very traditional example of *inspiration* in dreams. The drawings of the ex-Surrealist Giacometti reproduced here are part of the *recording and investigation* of a dream sequence. Schneemann's Kinetic Theatre is a *re-creation* of significant dream events; The Ting *re-enact* dream scenarios in a more formal way. The causal relationship between dream and art can be reversed: Gysin and Sommerville's Dreamachine *initiates or creates* the dream for the observer, and Hiller's Dream Mapping is an investigation of shared dreaming in which *the art process occurs in the dream state*, and only the documentation takes place in the waking state.

42 Alberto Giacometti: '. . . In spite of myself I began to express the dream differently. I tried to express in a more precise and striking way what had happened to me. . . . I wanted to say all this in a uniquely affective manner, to make certain points hallucinatory but without attempting to find the connection between them. . . . There was a contradiction between the affective way of expressing what I had found hallucinatory, and the series of facts which I wanted to describe. I found myself confused in a mass of events, places, and sensations. . . . I saw the design turn into an object: a disc with a radius of nearly two metres. . . . With strange pleasure I imagined myself walking on this disc – time – space – and reading the story before me. The freedom to begin when I liked, for instance to start off from the dream in October 1946 and, having gone all the way round, to land a few months earlier in front of the objects in front of my towel.' (Alberto Giacometti, 'The Dream, the Sphinx and the Death of T.', tr. Mary Hutchinson and David Wright, *X*, vol. 1, no. 1, London, 1959; first published in *Labyrinthe*, ed. Albert Skira, no. 2, Geneva, 1946.)

43 'The Ting enacts a flying dream by turning walls into floors.' (Dream Enactments, by The Ting, Great Britain, 1974.)

44 Carolee Schneemann: 'The source of all my work is poised between dreaming and waking. I keep pencils, pens, notebooks, tape recorder by the bed. In the past, I scrawled messages and drawings over the wall without even opening my eyes. At times I may forget the influence of a dream on a work and then later rediscover it.' (Up to and Including her Limits, by Carolee Schneemann, USA, 1974.)

45 Susan Hiller: 'Dream Mapping grew naturally out of earlier mapping pieces and an investigation called The Dream Seminar. . . . I've always been interested in notations of shared awareness, and this was an occasion for seven dreamers to diagram the dimensions, proportions, directions, and sense of dreams that occurred at a specific location and time. . . . The extent to which "subjective" psychic experiences and codes overlap is indicated by the heavy lines on the composite map. . . .' (Dream Mapping, by Susan Hiller, Great Britain, 1974.)

46 Brion Gysin and Ian Sommerville: 'The Dreamachine began as a simple means to investigate phenomena whose description excited our imaginations – our faculty of image-making which flicker was said to stimulate. . . . Maximum effect is achieved with a light of at least 100 watts when flicker plays over closed lids brought as close as possible to the cylinder. . . . The effects . . . continue to develop over a long period of time. . . . In the bigger machines . . . whole moving pictures are produced and seem to be in flux in three dimensions on a brilliant screen directly in front of the eyes.' (Brion Gysin, 'The Dreamachine', and Ian Sommerville, 'Flicker', *Olympia*, no. 2, Paris, 1962.) (The Dreamachine, by Brion Gysin and Ian Sommerville.)

43

44

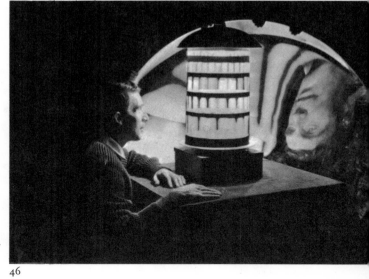

46

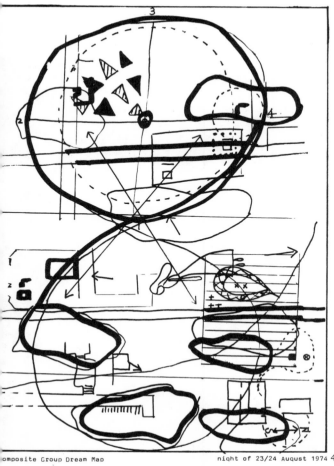

omposite Group Dream Map   night of 23/24 August 1974 45

Conscious dreams (1)

Astral projection, out-of-the-body experiences and lucid dreams are dream states in which the dreamer is conscious, or becomes conscious, during the dream. The first realization of this altered state of consciousness is described by Sylvan Muldoon: 'The first projection . . . in which I became conscious was a dream projection. I dreamed that I was walking along a dusty road. It was a sweltering hot day. I was thirsty but could find no place to drink . . . There was a windmill! I hurried as fast as I could to the tank below it – but it was dry! I looked up at the wheel above me and saw that it was not turning, and, knowing that it would pump water if the wheel were turned, . . . I began to climb the ladder of the windmill. Just as I reached the top the wheel began to turn rapidly and, catching my clothing, threw me outward through the air, for I could see that I was speeding toward a river near my home, and that I should probably get a drink there. Soon I was by the river and on my knees drinking. It was at that moment that I became clearly conscious, and I found myself in the astral body on the bank of the river . . . at a spot where I often went fishing.'

The themes of ascent (the ladder), flying (moving outward) and becoming conscious (waking) are all present in this account.

Whether or not the astral body has an ontological reality, or a quasi-ontological reality (in that it exists because consciousness can perceive itself or conceive of itself only as embodied in an image, even if non-material); and whether or not ontology itself has any meaning in what is possibly an illusory world of non-materiality or non-objectivity, the concept of the astral body, or spirit-body, or *ba*, is found in many cultures.

47 Egyptian initiates believed that human nature was composed of six elements, three material (body, name, shadow) and three spiritual (*ka, ba, akh*). The *ba*, always represented as a jabiru-bird bearing the face of the deceased, was thought to leave the body during dreams and at death, remaining conscious, autonomous and lucid in the afterworld. (*Ba* and corpse being embalmed, from a stele, Egypt, 3rd–1st c. BC, Ny Carlsberg Glyptothek, Copenhagen; see pl. 28 and p. 75.)

The complete journey that Muldoon began has been described in detail by Milarepa (see p. 14) and others. The Chinese 'stages of meditation' illustrated here are closely related to the Tibetan *Chos-drug*. The inspirational texts accompanying the illustrations finish by noting: 'the shapes formed by the spirit fire are only empty lines and forms'. (From *Hui Ming Ching*, reproduced in C. G. Jung, *Alchemical Studies*, London, 1967.)

48 'Stage 1: Gathering the Light.'

49 'Stage 2: Origin of a new being in the place of power.'

50 'Stage 3: Separation of the spirit-body for independent existence.'

51 'Stage 4: The centre in the midst of conditions.'

The stages of projection of the astral body. (From Sylvan Muldoon and Hereward Carrington, *The Projection of the Astral Body*, New York, 1929.)

52 'The phantom, slightly out of coincidence.'

53 'The phantom lying in the air above the physical body. The phantom sometimes uprights here.'

54 'Arrows show the route the phantom takes in projection. This is the position the phantom often occupies, prior to a flying dream, which is followed by a falling dream. Phantom often uprights here.'

55 'Phantom projected and upright within cord-activity-range.'

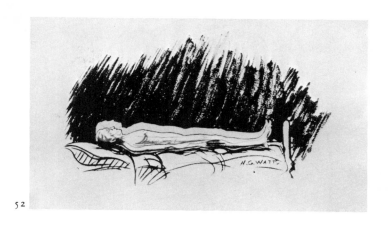

52

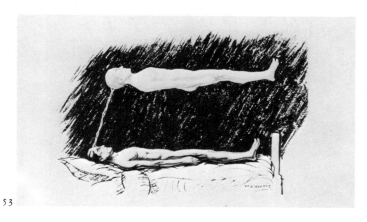

53

54

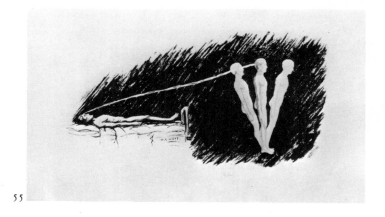

55

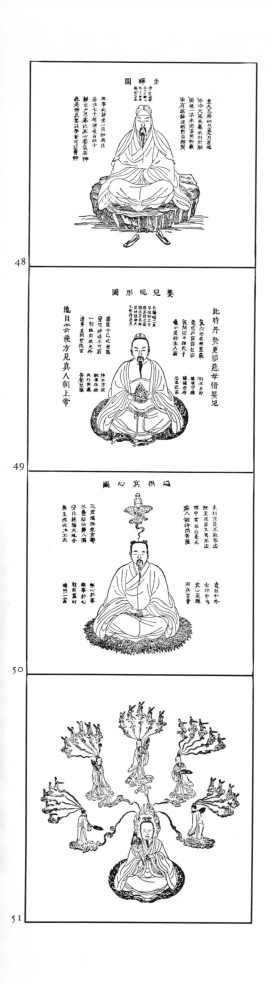

48

49

50

51

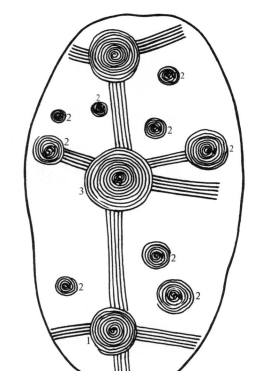

56

57

94

Conscious dreams (2)

The Australian concept of the Dreaming or the Dreamtime, an era in which the mythical ancestors of the aborigines live, is not thought of as a time that is past, but as a contemporary situation which validates the events of today, functioning as a kind of charter for social actions. The subtlety of this concept is exemplified in the material manifestations called *churinga*, which are at once the spiritual body of a person and a sacred occult map of Dreamtime events. The *churinga* represent the mystical bonds between humans and their mythic ancestors, and may also be described as constituting an aspect of the supernatural, deathless body of an individual's mother. They are, virtually, notations on the nature of the spiritual and material worlds seen simultaneously from the points of view of individual and collective consciousness.

56, 57 The map meanings of this *churinga* have been described in these terms: 'At a place valled Ngapatjimbi (1), a number of grasshoppers came out of the ground, flew up into the air and went back to the ground again. There they multiplied, and after the next rain came out in other places (2). They flew up into the air and came down as men. These men went to Wantaugara (3) and, going into a cave, they turned into *churinga*.' The parallel lines linking the circles represent paths made by the grasshoppers by breaking down grass and leaves. The pairs of short lines are their prints in the sand. Nagapatjimbi and Wantaugara are scared sites in the desert about fifty miles north of MacDonnell Ranges, central Australia. (*Churinga*, central Australia, Museum of Mankind, London.)

58 Achok, a Malaysian Senoi, drew this diagram of himself dreaming in the shaman's hut. The central point represents Achok; the spokes are leaves forming the cone-shaped roof; the circumference of the circle is the rim of the round floor. All Senoi who attain the highest level of initiation build a hut of the same sort and isolate themselves in it, hoping to achieve total possession by their spiritual guides. All of them represent the experience in identical diagrams, which symbolize wholeness and the complete integration of internal and external reality. The diagrams show the Self at the spiritual centre of the world, which can be anywhere. The structure of the psyche as defined by the Senoi is duplicated in the structure of the shaman's hut, or temple, and, by analogy, echoed in the design of the entire cosmos. In Senoi terminology, the five segments of the circle represent the five 'souls' which are aspects of every human being, although their potential remains in abeyance unless consciously developed. (Drawing by Achok, from copy after Kilton Stewart, 'Magico-Religious Beliefs and Practices . . .', unpub. thesis, University of London, 1948.)

59 According to Tibetan Buddhist teaching, the centre of human consciousness is empty and beyond all limiting definitions. The centre is surrounded by five sheaths which, in ever-increasing density, crystallize around the inner point of our being. The densest of these sheaths is the physical body, built up through nutrition; next is the subtle or etheric body, nourished by breath; next is the thought body or personality, formed by active thought; the fourth is the body of potential spiritual consciousness; the fifth is the body of blissful, universal consciousness, experienced only in a state of enlightenment. The development of full lucidity in waking life and dream life is an essential step towards understanding the interpenetration and relationship of these aspects of the Self. (From Anagarika Govinda, *Foundations of Tibetan Mysticism*, London, 1960.)

60 Aranda *churinga*, central Australia. (Museum of Mankind, London.)

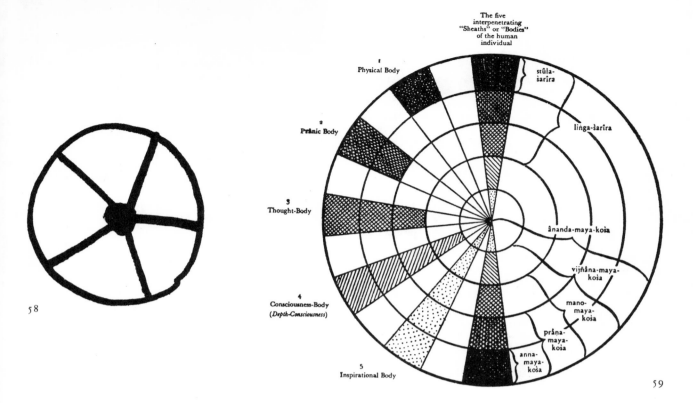

58

The five
interpenetrating
"Sheaths" or "Bodies"
of the human
individual

1
Physical Body

stûla-
śarîra

2
Prânic Body

liṅga-śarîra

3
Thought-Body

ânanda-maya-kośa

vijñâna-maya-
kośa

mano-
maya-
kośa

prâna-
maya-
kośa

anna-
maya-
kośa

4
Consciousness-Body
(*Depth-Consciousness*)

5
Inspirational Body

59

60

95

Sources of quotations

Uitoto creation myth: tr. Margot Astrov, *The Winged Serpent. American Indian prose and poetry*, New York, 1946.

Chuang-tsu: tr. Arthur Waley, *Madly Singing in the Mountains*, London, 1970.

Carlos Castaneda, *Journey to Ixtlan*, London, 1973.

Mircea Eliade, *Myths, Dreams and Mysteries*, London, 1960.

Australian statement: quoted by W. E. H. Stanner, 'The Dreaming', in. T. A. G. Hungerford (ed.), *Australian Signpost*, Melbourne, 1956.

Bhagwan Shree Rajneesh, *The Internal Revolution*, Bombay, 1973.

Heraclitus, tr. Philip Wheelwright, *Heraclitus*, Princeton, 1959.

Aristotle, 'On Prophecy in Sleep,' tr. W. S. Hett, *On the Soul: Parva Naturalia, On Breath*, Boston, 1936.

Artemidorus, *Oneirocritica*, tr. R. Wood, London, 1644.

Najmoddin Kobra, Shamsoddin Lahiji, and Ibn 'Arabi: tr. Henry Corbin, 'The Visionary Dream in Islamic Spirituality,' *The Dream and Human Societies*, G. E. von Grunebaum and Roger Callois (eds), Berkeley, 1966.

Kilton R. Stewart, 'Dream Theory in Malaya,' *Altered States of Consciousness*, Charles T. Tart (ed.), New York, 1969.

Father Fremin: quoted in *Black Gown and Red Skins*, E. Kenton (ed.), London, 1956.

Smohalla: Herbert J. Spinden, *The Nez Perce Indians*, American Anthropological Association Memoires, Lancaster, 1908.

Lost Star, and Papago Foot: Leslie Spier, *Yuman tribes of the Gila River*, University of Chicago Publications in Anthropology, Ethnographical Series, Chicago, 1933.

The Thirteen Principal Upanishads, tr. R. E. Hume, Oxford, 1931.

Rechung's Life of Milarepa, tr. Lama Kazi Dawa-Sandup, *Tibet's Great Yogi, Milarepa*, W. Y. Evans-Wentz (ed.), Oxford, 1928.

Sigmund Freud, *The Interpretation of Dreams*, tr. James Strachey, London, 1954.

André Breton, *Surrealists on Art*, Lucy Lippard (ed.), New York, 1970.

C. G. Jung, *Modern Man in Search of a Soul*, London, 1933.

C. G. Jung, *Memories, Dreams and Reflections*, London, 1963.

June Singer, *Boundaries of the Soul*, London, 1973.

C. G. Jung, *Symbols of Transformation*, Collected Works, vol. 5, London, 1956.

Brave Buffalo, and Teal Duck: Francis Densmore, *Teton Sioux Music*, Bureau of American Ethnology, Washington, 1918.

Meckawigabau: Francis Densmore, *Chippewa Music*, Bureau of American Ethnology, Washington, 1910.

Aristides: E. R. Dodds, *The Greeks and the Irrational*, Boston, 1957.

Black Elk: *Black Elk Speaks*, as told through John G. Neihardt, Lincoln, 1961.

Norman Malcolm, *Dreaming*, Studies in Philosophical Psychology, London, 1959.

Frederick van Eeden, *A Study of Dreams*, Proceedings of the Society for Psychical Research, London, 1913.

C. G. Jung, *Alchemical Studies*, Collected Works, vol. 13, London, 1967.

Robert A. Monroe, *Journeys out of the Body*, New York, 1973.

Charles T. Tart, 'The "High" Dream', *Altered States of Consciousness*, Charles T. Tart (ed.), New York, 1969.

Claudio Naranjo and Robert E. Ornstein, *On the Psychology of Meditation*, London, 1972.

Hervey de Saint-Denis, *Les Rêves et les moyens de les diriger*, Paris, 1867.

Sylvan Muldoon and Hereward Carrington, *The Projection of the Astral Body*, New York, 1929.

General sources and recommended further reading

Henri Bergson, *Dreams*, London, 1914.

Raymond de Becker, *The Understanding of Dreams*, London, 1968.

Joseph Campbell (ed.), *Myths, Dreams and Religion*, New York, 1970.

Carlos Castaneda, *Tales of Power*, New York, 1974.

George Devereux (ed.), *Psychoanalysis and the Occult*, London, 1974.

J. W. Dunne, *An Experiment with Time*, London, 1927.

Mircea Eliade, *Yoga, Immortality and Freedom*, Bollingen Series, Princeton, 1969.

Ann Faraday, *Dream Power*, New York, 1972.

Celia Green, *Lucid Dreams*, Proceedings of the Institute for Psychophysical Research, London, 1968.

Frederick Greenwood, *Imagination in Dreams*, London, 1894.

C. Kerényi, *Asklepios*, London, 1960.

S. G. M. Lee and A. R. Mayer (eds.), *Dreams and Dreaming*, London, 1973.

Montague Ullman, Stanley Krippner and Alan Vaughn, *Dream Telepathy*, London, 1973.

Objects in the plates are reproduced by courtesy of the following: Albany, NY., New York State Museum 35; Copenhagen, Nationalmuseum 38; D. Coxhead and S. Hiller 48; Ferrara, Pinacoteca 36; Campbell Grant 5; London, The Archbishop of Canterbury and the Trustees of the Lambeth Palace Library 1, British Library 30, 49, British Museum 2, 3, 21, 28, Museum of Mankind 39, Tate Gallery 11, Victoria and Albert Museum 22, 29; Ajit Mookerjee 4, 41, 46; New York, Metropolitan Museum of Art 20, 27, Museum of the American Indian, Heye Foundation 12, 43, 44, 45; Paris, Bibliothèque Nationale 10, 25, 33, 34; Edward C. Peach 17, 18; Philadelphia Museum of Art 23; Santa Fe, Museum of Navajo Ceremonial Art 42; George E. Schoenkopf Gallery, New York 13; Sotheby & Co., London 8; Strasbourg, Musée des Beaux-Arts 14; Venice, Galleria dell'Accademia 32; Vienna, Kunsthistorisches Museum 9; Washington DC, The Smithsonian Institution, Freer Gallery of Art 26.

The authors would like to thank the following friends for the loan of specific visual or textual material used in this book: Michael Fior, Tamara Kaddishman, Signe Lie, David Maclagan, Christina Toren and Max Yeh; *and the Gardner Centre for the Arts, University of Sussex, for the use of their facilities while this book was being written.*

61 Tibetan talisman in the form of a scorpion, used by the dreamer for protection against the forces of evil that may appear in dreams. (From L. A. Waddell, *The Buddhism of Tibet*, London, 1895.)